Reflections on

Evolutionary Activism

Essays, poems and prayers

from an emerging field of sacred social change

by

Tom Atlee

ISBN 1449597955

Published by
Evolutionary Action Press
PO Box 10374
Eugene, OR 97440

Available online at
EvolutionaryActivism.com

BACK COVER SYMBOL: The symbol in the lower left corner is the co-intelligence symbol, described at http://co-intelligence.org/CIsymbol.html.

PHOTO CREDIT: The photograph on the cover is an edited Hubble Space Telescope image of the M101 Galaxy (also known as the Pinwheel Galaxy), which is twice the size of our own Milky Way, and about 24 million light years away. Credit for the original image goes to: NASA, ESA, K. Kuntz (JHU), F. Bresolin (University of Hawaii), J. Trauger (Jet Propulsion Lab), J. Mould (NOAO), Y.-H. Chu (University of Illinois, Urbana), and STScI

To the memory of

Thomas Berry

and

Julian Huxley

There's a joke among cosmologists
that romantics are made of stardust,
but cynics are made of the nuclear waste of worn-out stars.
Sure enough, the complex atoms coming out of supernovas
can be seen either way,
but these atoms introduce into matter the possibility of complexity,
and complexity allows the possibility of life and intelligence.
To call them nuclear waste is like
calling consumer goods the waste products of factories.
A cosmology can be a source of tremendous inspirational
and even healing power,
or it can transform a people into slaves or automatons
and squash their universe into obsession with the next meal
or with trivial entertainment.
The choice of what attitude the twenty-first century will adopt
toward the new universe
may be the greatest opportunity of our time.

— Joel Primack and Nancy Abrams

We are the product of the process of evolution, and ... we have become the process itself, through the emergence and evolution of our consciousness, our awareness, our capacity to imagine and anticipate the future, and to choose from among alternatives.

Jonas Salk

Table of Contents

Prologue

How I stumbled into my evolutionary epiphany

I've been an activist all my life, but something strange and profound happened to me early in the summer of 2005. I wish I could remember what day it was, because it was a watershed in my life. I'd like to celebrate it every year. Instead, I just find myself living it every day.

One of my projects back then was helping former evangelical preacher and sustainability organizer Michael Dowd organize what he called "an evolutionary salon" in May.[1] We convened about three dozen evolutionary scientists, spiritual leaders and social activists for five days of open exploration,

---

[1] For more information about Michael Dowd see *michaeldowd.org*. For more information about evolutionary salons, see *thegreatstory .org/ev-salon.html*.

with interesting results. After the gathering, I returned to my life, as I do after so many conferences.

A month later an hour before bedtime, I sat at my desk in Eugene, Oregon, to watch a video of Michael and his science-writer wife Connie Barlow explaining evolution as a sacred, meaningful story. They were claiming that if we understand this story deeply enough, it will transform how we think, feel, and act in the world.

I expected to become better informed—and I was. What I didn't expect was to be transformed. Which I also was— quite suddenly and startlingly.

I was listening to Connie explain to a group of teachers how *all* the hydrogen atoms in the water that is everywhere in and around us were created shortly after the Big Bang 13.7 billion years ago. That's *old!*

I looked at the water bottle on my desk. It seemed different somehow, vaguely miraculous, filled with the most ancient things in the universe. I took a drink, and remembered that my body is about 70 percent water. The idea that that much of me is directly connected to the Big Bang gave me a very strange feeling.

Connie was continuing her enthusiastic narrative: The original hydrogen was invisibly, thinly spread throughout space. Picking at each vague thickening in this ghostly universe, gravity slowly pulled each cosmic cloud-colony of hydrogen closer and tighter together until some of them suddenly burst into atomic fire as the first stars. I had only a moment to realize there was once a time of infinite darkness with no stars.

But Connie was moving on, describing how red giant stars have for billions of years been using hydrogen to forge more atoms—among them carbon, oxygen, and nitrogen. These atoms join hydrogen to compose most of living, breathing nature (including us) here on Earth. She explained how all the heavier elements—including other life-essentials like calcium and magnesium—were minted in searing supernova explosions—each one as bright as a whole galaxy—that hurled those tiny atomic building-blocks of planets and life across millions of miles of space. Dying red giants and supernovas, like giant cosmic seed-pods bursting, are our ancestors.

Based on these facts, Connie calmly pointed out—with a glint in her eye—that we are, scientifically speaking, stardust. There's nothing esoteric about it. We are made of the stuff of stars—we are all echoes of the Big Bang—and so is everyone and everything around us. Ancient stars had to live and die before our Earth could be born. You can make a star out of just hydrogen gas, but you need heartier stuff to make a planet.

So that's our Genesis. Today, when we look out into "space", we are actually looking back into time, at stars and galaxies as they were when the dinosaurs roamed, when the first bacteria formed, when Earth was an airless molten ball growing ever larger through the thunderous impact of meteors, and even eons before that into the earliest coalescings of grandparent stars and galaxies...

And just as it is *me* as a whole—not just my eyeballs— that is looking at this room, Connie enthused, so it is that we are the universe, the unfolding story of evolution itself, newly aware of itself, peering at itself through our eyes, through our telescopes, through layers of fossils and rocks, awe-struck, wondering...

Then it happened: One moment I was watching and listening to Connie saying all this. Then—I can't explain what happened next except that my body and chair and computer and desk and house and neighborhood and city and world *became* stardust—not static specks, but a slow-motion, incredibly complex and changing wave of evolving star-stuff unfolding into tomorrow and tomorrow and tomorrow... There was no separation between me and everything else. We all *were that*—and it was becoming more alive and conscious by the minute. I could feel in every cell of my body-mind an urge to become more alive, conscious, responsive and engaged, to join wholeheartedly, whole-spiritedly in this great wave of evolutionary unfolding of which I was suddenly, newly a conscious part...

> *Everything became a slow-motion tsunami of evolving star-stuff*

I assure you this was not in any way "an idea". This was a vividly lived experience, as real to me as my normal sense of the world. I experienced us all as the living face of evolution now.

From that moment till now, nothing has been the same. I don't *live* in that consciousness, but I can touch it any time I want, and I am learning to *live into it*. I can't shake the cer-

tainty that it *means* something very important for what we
do here and now.

Having had this experience, I "got it" why Michael and
Connie had been traveling around the country for years, living out of their large white van, teaching and preaching a
meaningful, sacred understanding of evolution in hundreds
of churches, schools, and community organizations. Evolution is, indeed, a Great Story of unprecedented power. That
power is obscured by the way it is usually taught—as a
merely mechanistic mutation-and-natural-selection dinosaur-
and-monkey related thing that happened in some distant
time and place. In my epiphany I woke up to how Connie
and Michael saw evolution: as a potent, incredibly meaningful and alive tsunami of the Universe surging right now
through our lives and global events. Indeed, evolution *is* our
lives and global events. We *are* it—or rather, we are that part
of it that is happening right now in our human world and a
major part of the evolution of our planet.

I saw vividly how this realization would help us better
engage with the evolutionary challenges and opportunities
we face right now. I felt evolution calling us to apply what it
has given us—our peculiar human consciousness and our social systems—to the evolutionary project and to our own
survival and thrival in it. I saw that as more of us realize
these things at deeper levels—which is already happening—a
new movement is slowly emerging, a movement of tremendous depth and breadth and import.

The first Evolutionary Salon had, surprisingly, concluded
with a vision of "a movement for the conscious evolution of

increasingly conscious social systems." It seemed to me that to the extent social systems were conscious, they would not destroy themselves and their world but would instead become joyfully aware wisdom cultures, harmonious with one another and their Earth-home. I, who had earlier participated in the salon's discovery of that vision, had now had an evolutionary epiphany revealing what that vision meant. I had seen in one flash that it was not only possible but right in the flow of unfolding evolution. In my years of research since then, I have seen even deeper into that truth, with profound implications for activism.

As happens with anyone who has a powerful epiphany, I became entranced with what would happen if millions of people came to see what I had been privileged to see.

I could feel my world shifting. I went on a retreat during October and November 2005. Among many other activities, I read, wrote, had long talks with friends and colleagues (including three days with Michael Dowd), took a class in Appreciative Inquiry, and spent two and a half days alone in a yurt meditating, listening to my heart and the world, reflecting on my life, seeking guidance about where I might most strategically put my energies.

During that retreat I realized that my life now had to include inviting others into this remarkable evolutionary understanding, finding ways to *live* the truth it had revealed to me, and doing what I could to manifest the evolutionary activist movement vision that had emerged five months earlier.

These realizations did not result in my leaving the co-intelligence work I'd been engaged in for almost two decades. Rather, I saw that, at its heart, the co-intelligence work had always been about catalyzing the conscious evolution of civilization. Indeed, it was about nurturing the capacity of societies to consciously evolve themselves. I hadn't seen that so clearly before. My epiphany placed my co-intelligence work within a larger, more com-pelling, and potentially far more powerful context: a social change movement grounded in the trans-formative power of Evolution, just as Gandhi's *Satyagraha* ("truth force") movement was grounded in the transformative power of Truth and Martin Luther King's nonviolent civil rights movement was grounded in the transformative power of Love. In such movements, activists don't so much push change as nurture the courage to live as strategic channels for a larger transformative Power working through them to invite, inspire and disturb society into greater aware-ness and change.

Social change movements that channel the transformative power of Truth, Love and Evolution

So now my life is inhabited by ever-changing evolution-ary activist questions, like:

How can we—you and I—engage more consciously with the evolutionary unfolding of which we—and our comput-ers, our governments, our movements, our world and our universe—are all naturally miraculous expressions and ac-tive participants?

How can we more consistently see ourselves as the living face of evolution now—with everything at stake, and everything possible—with billions of years of experience embedded in every atom of our lives.

I keep seeing signs that we are waking up to this together. I suspect that, as we do, we will discover increasingly remarkable things about who we are, who we could be, and what we could do together.

Archimedes famously said that if he had a long enough lever and a place to stand, he could move the world. The evolutionary lever is 13.7 billion years long and, grounded in the realities of our times and our emerging understandings from both science and spirit, we can now join with the Creative Power that has always moved the cosmos and is even now moving our world toward what it will, with our help, become...

Introduction

This book is coming into being right now because humanity's situation requires a miracle so vast and evolving that it begins to look like the miracle that began the universe in the first place. Perhaps more to the point, the required miracle will, by necessity, be a new chapter in the miraculous evolutionary unfolding that brought us to where we are now.

This book looks at "evolution" as the story and process of all developments in the universe up until now—what some call "big history" or "a deep time perspective". We are part of that great story and that process. We are now at a point in the story where we need to wake up to the deep-time reality in which we're participating—at least if we wish to continue as part of the story.

This will not be easy.

In this new evolutionary chapter, human consciousness, wisdom, and choice will play a greater role in the evolutionary process and in sustaining the shared life of humanity and the natural world. This does not mean humans will play a controlling role. Rather, we will tap the wisdom of evolu-

tion and natural process to become wise participants and
partners in this unfolding miracle, acutely aware that it *is* a
miracle.

Evolutionary science now shares with many religions
the understanding that life is a miracle, at least in this sense:
Cosmologists now suggest that there are so many other ways
our universe and our planet could have begun and developed that would have been unfriendly to life, that it is a
miracle anything or any of us exist at all. The world we live
in is, speaking scientifically as well as poetically, a mind-
bogglingly improbable miracle. The continued existence of
humanity may now require a miracle of that magnitude—a
miracle brought about by us as evolutionary activists.

In one sense humanity's situation is nothing new. What
we're doing is not sustainable. We're consuming and fouling
our life support systems in ways that make extinction increasingly likely. Yet species have been going extinct for billions of years, some of them by consuming and fouling their
environments. At one point before us, this dynamic almost
destroyed all life on Earth. Before oxygen-breathing animals
showed up, the original photosynthetic organisms churned
out so much oxygen that the whole Earth started to corrode
around them, becoming toxic and taking life to the edge of
total breakdown. Sound familiar?

Consider how we've done it. As conscious beings we've
raised extinction preparations to a fine art. We break through
natural checks and balances to get our way on virtually all
fronts, seeing every challenge to our dominance as a problem to solve, and solving it. We've solved our way further

and further out on the limb of social and natural capacity—
all the while growing our population, our consumption and
our assumptions about how valuable and exceptional we
humans are—that we are exponentially exceeding the carrying capacity of this very finite branch upon which we still
insist on venturing further and further. It is no accident that
the language describing our situation increasingly uses the
word "break"—breakdown and breakthrough.

This is where the miracle comes in. The miracle is the
other side of the coin of our dire situation. That other side is
our consciousness of what is happening to us, and of its significance. The very fact that I can write about this in evolutionary terms—that we face extinction—is something new
under the sun. Three hundred years ago we didn't even know
about extinction.

*We are the first species to know we are part of the Great Story
of evolution.* We are the first species to know that we could go
extinct. And, most importantly, we are the first species to
know that we could prevent that extinction by doing certain
things. Finally, we are the first species to know that if we did
those things—if we transformed the way we relate to our
environment so that we could maintain a sustainable fit with
the world we live in—we would have become not only a
new creation but a *conscious* evolutionary force. We would be
a part of evolution that had suddenly awakened and become
conscious of itself and what it was doing, and then was making conscious, informed choices about what to do next—over
and over, learning and evolving each step of the way, just

like evolution has been doing more or less unconsciously for billions of years.

This book is for those of us who wish to wake up to this unprecedented fact and take evolutionary responsibility for the fate of humanity, our civilization, and our planet. It is for those of us who see that such conscious evolutionary responsibility does not mean managing and controlling everything— manipulating genes and machines and people and nature to make them do what we think needs to be done. Rather it means learning how to partner with the 13.7 billion year old wisdom of nature, especially the wise ways of evolution, the mother of all change, all process, all innovation, and all life. It is for those of us willing and ready to work with, for, and as the evolutionary process of which we have always been part.

We are becoming a conscious evolutionary force

In short, this book is for anyone who sees that becoming *conscious evolutionary activists* is not only necessary, but is the beginning of one of the most miraculous journeys in the history of the universe. This new evolutionary story involves an awesome responsibility, an inspiring mission rich with tantalizing possibilities, remarkable companionship, and a deep reverence for life and for the ancient creative Power that has always been with us and among us, and that we now call upon to work with us and through us as conscious beings.

This book does not show up in a vacuum. There are many change agents even now doing work that is vital for creating a sustainable, consciously evolving civilization. The only difference between them and the vision in this book is that they don't think of their work in evolutionary terms. They do not seek wisdom from evolutionary dynamics or inspiration from evolution's sacred Great Story, nor do they identify themselves with evolution itself.

On the other hand, a loose-knit community of diverse conscious evolutionaries already exists. It includes everything from meditators evolving their consciousness to transhumanists evolving the machines they see merging with us to become the new dominant species. It includes integral thinkers who call for us to attend to the development of individuals and collectives, inside and out, and it includes visionaries who see us headed towards unification with God.

Into this mix, this book invites a vision of a movement for the conscious evolution of increasingly conscious social systems—a movement of activists dedicated to calling forth new social systems. These are new forms of economics, politics, governance, and cultural stories that are increasingly aligned with the realities of nature and humanity. These conscious evolutionary activists realize that such social systems would not constitute an ideal utopian state, but would rather be endlessly imperfect, like the universe, yet capable of their own ongoing evolution into greater wisdom, more beauty and complexity, and more evolutionary fitness. These conscious evolutionary activists are not utopians because they know that the only way a civilization woven of such systems could succeed would be to honor diversity, disturbance, and change as signs of health and resources brimming with possibility. We're talking about responsive vitality, not perfection and ideological correctness.

When I first felt the calling to write this book, I thought it would be something more like the book that launched Taoism, the *Tao Teh Ching* by Lao Tzu, a poetic expression of the underlying intelligence of nature and how it applies to human life and society. But life got in the way, and I ended up writing many evolutionary essays and poems in between the challenges life brought to me. 2008-2009 brought signs that a profound shift was underway—the meltdown of the economy, journalism, and other status-quo systems; increasingly dire news about climate change and energy; the intense political dance of healing, possibility, polarization and frustration accompanying Obama's emergence; colleagues collapsing in sobs about the future. These and other rapidly emerging, highly charged phenomena have given me a sense that we are on the launching pad for a very intense evolutionary moment, ripe with potential trauma and possibility.

I no longer feel I can wait to write a book from scratch. The meme of evolutionary activism wants to escape the confines of my universe into the wider society, to seek its fortune in the maelstrom, with the chance of playing a useful role in the miracle that so much needs and wants to happen. I feel called to get out a book quickly, using mostly what I have already written. That is the book you hold in your hand or are reading on your computer. It is self-published because publishing through traditional means would take a year or more, and the time to invite this new form of activism is *now*.

To a great extent, this book is a body of essays that can each be read independently. Written from the same field of inspiration, they are, in a sense, fractal or holographic: Each contains many parts of the whole, seen from a different angle. Thus you can scan through the book for ideas that catch your attention, reading here and there, without fearing you are missing foundations laid earlier. The book is also organized so you can read through it and sense a coherent flow. The poems, with their own independent integrity, are positioned to encourage deeper feeling and reflection on adjacent chapters and on the evolutionary perspective as a whole.

Finally, for better and worse, this book is not a master plan for evolutionary activism. It is barely a beginning, a sketch pad, a napkin on the table of our conversations about activism and evolution. I see it as an invitation to co-create a diverse field of activist ideas and projects informed by evolutionary science, inspired by the sacred evolutionary story, and grounded in the reality that we are all evolutionary pioneers right now, standing together at a crossroads. This book is my spark, in search of other sparks, in search of tinder.

I don't have a plan. I am not an organizer. I will do my best to make space to talk about all this, to explore how it might develop most usefully. I would love to be a thinking partner in whatever happens next.

Blessings on the Journey.

Tom Atlee
November 26, 2009

Stardust Settles on Earth to Learn

Exploded starfields
mingled gravitationally, geologically, weatherly
into a planet we could live on,
our Mother.

And then a long, long, long time passed,
during which untold lives and places
created and erased
one another.

And thus we came to be,
along with all the rest
of what we see
as solid reality
instead of realizing what it is:
a shared learning space
for the smallest creatures
and the greatest natures,
churning out lessons, classrooms, field trips,
end times and beginnings,
and final exams, one after the other.
sister and brother,
the least and the best.

And this miracle moment,
this time of all horror and hope,
this is our test.

| ✳ |

Reflections on

Evolution and Creation

Chapter One

Evolution 2.0:
A Big History that embraces
all the sciences

This book is about the implications of evolutionary science and spirituality for social change activism. It arises from an evolutionary perspective now widely shared by the scientific community. Here's one way to summarize that perspective:

Progressive evolutionary change has been going on since the Big Bang. It sped up as life evolved. It is now unfolding most rapidly and obviously here on Earth in the human realm, especially in the evolution of culture, social systems, technology, and human consciousness—and in humanity's impacts on the world.

Social change activism plays a role in changing human attitudes, behaviors, and society itself. It is an intrinsic part of the human evolutionary process.

As a life-long activist exploring this evolutionary world-view, I wondered if we could combine scientific knowledge of evolutionary dynamics with spiritual inspiration from the deep-time evolutionary story to generate more coherent, effective and meaningful forms of social change activism. I compiled this book to share what I've found so far. I see the book itself—and the fact that you are reading it—as part of the evolutionary process beginning to wake up to what it is doing and, with delight, doing it ever more consciously among us and through us.

For those of us already engaged with evolutionary science and spirituality, I believe the opportunity to apply the evolutionary perspective to making the world a better place —to actually make a positive contribution to the evolution of civilization—adds a powerful new dimension to our role in the evolutionary story.

For those not familiar with the sacred evolutionary worldview, the Prologue and these first two chapters will serve as an introduction to my own understanding and love of it, which will surface again and again in these pages.

To begin here, I will share some background on the context within which evolutionary activism emerged, specifically, some history of how we humans have evolved in our understanding of the idea of evolution and our deepening relationship to it. When I look over this history, evolutionary activism seems like a natural outgrowth of what has come before, more like a ripening or unfolding than just one more grand idea.

As our understanding of evolution grows, it is becoming increasingly obvious that we can and should apply our evolutionary knowledge to society, so that our social systems become more deeply aligned with the realities of nature and with who we are as people. Evolutionary understandings can help us evolve into wise societies whose vitality both arises from *and supports* the whole of life.

A history of the term "evolution"

"E-volution" derives from Latin roots meaning "to roll out", as in "to unfold." For many centuries "evolution" meant the progressive, often gradual development of something, especially from a simple to a more complex form. Most modern dictionaries include that definition.

Evolution, as it is discussed in this book, covers the full unfolding of the universe, active even today. Evolution plays out at every scale and in every aspect of life, albeit at profoundly different speeds—and often with different dynamics—in different realms. It is not just change, but change that builds on itself, with the new and novel arising from that which already exists.

The evolutionary journey itself may or may not have a destination, but it does tend to have a direction—although not necessarily a linear one. It often meanders and backtracks, with interesting offshoots, plateaus and dead-ends. Also, we almost always find many developmental stages co-existing in the same person, community, society, world, and universe. Bacteria are everywhere. Shakespeare, Gandhi and Mother Theresa all had reptilian urges. The most common thing in the universe is also its simplest: hydrogen. Just because a house is more complex than a brick doesn't mean the bricks aren't there along with the house.

In the big long view, however, a clear look back at any evolutionary sequence shows it unfolding in a particular way or building something up. We see this not only in the evolution of life, but in everyday expressions like "the evolution of the internet" or "the evolution of Sino-American relations."

Interestingly enough, Charles Darwin only used the word *evolution* on the last page of his watershed book, *On the Origin of Species*. He avoided it because, in his time, it meant something *destined and prepared in order to develop*, whereas he was promoting a relatively random vision of natural selection that happened in real time, according to how well an organism's inheritable characteristics happened to fit the demands of the changing environment it happened to be in.

Our understanding of evolution has been evolving for 300 years

Darwin's theory has proven remarkably robust, but we now know it doesn't quite embrace the whole story. Today, most living evolutionary biologists acknowledge that a sort of "predestination" arises from Darwinian randomness: Certain widespread environmental conditions like light and air evoke functional adaptations like eyes and wings. Indeed, numerous examples of such *convergent evolution* have shown up independently in diverse branches of life and are thus now seen as relatively inevitable, under the right conditions.

Furthermore, we now know that the same genes will bring forth different forms, functions and behaviors in different environmental conditions, and that this range of variation is itself influenced by the range of environments those genes have experienced in the past. Obviously, there is far more than pure randomness going on here. Or perhaps we should rather say that randomness has a designing intelligence of its own that we did not foresee—a designing intelligence that foreshadows our own responsive intelligence.

Darwin's work ended up shifting humanity's meaning of the word evolution to align more with his views. In today's popular mind it conjures up random changes in organisms, with new species arising from natural selection, culminating in humans as the height of elegant complexity—even if the jury is still out on our species' ultimate evolutionary success.

Darwinism became not only the epitome of evolutionary thought for many decades, but was exemplary of a larger shift in thinking that has been underway for about 300 years: Breaking out of a religion-based worldview that saw everything created all at once and unchanging since the beginning (or at least designed for a desired developmental path), scientists and philosophers began suggesting that things were not always as they are now, that they required no designer to evolve into new forms, and that our world was a good deal older than previously thought.

By the 1600s (and earlier in China and Greece) European geologists were puzzling over marine fossils in mountains. In 1795 James Hutton, influenced by medieval Islamic geologists, suggested that our current earth structures had been formed by dynamics like erosion and uplift, acting over eons. Starting in 1830 Charles Lyell promoted the idea that geologic processes have been going on continuously and slowly since Earth's formation, extending the age of the Earth into millions of years. Darwin explored such geological inquiries before beginning his biological work, and was strongly influenced by Lyell's sense of deep time.

When radioactive dating techniques were developed in the 20th century (based on the half-life of radioactive elements), more accurate estimates of the ages of rocks clarified just how old they were: some have been around for billions of years. And in the 1960s, our understanding of Earth's geologic evolutionary story was dramatically advanced by the discovery of plate tectonics, which described the dynamics underlying changes in the earth's crust.

Biological evolutionary understandings emerged quite naturally from geological evolutionary understandings, because life emerged from the geosphere. When geologists found deeply embedded fossils of seashells hundreds of miles from the sea, they started thinking about the history of Earth in new ways. But it wasn't until the 20th century that evolutionary thinking fully expanded both backward to the beginning of time and forward into culture, ultimately embracing and influencing every scientific field.

Take astronomy. The existence of galaxies outside our Milky Way was barely imagined even a century ago. Their presence was only verified and catalogued in the 1930s by Edwin Hubble with the Mt. Wilson telescope. Hubble also found compelling evidence that distant galaxies were moving away from us faster than nearby galaxies, supporting what became known as the Big Bang theory that the universe had begun as an explosion from a common central point. Discovery of cosmic microwave background radiation in the 1960s further supported the Big Bang narrative.

In the 1930s-60s space turned into time. As we learned about the astronomical distances involved with objects that were becoming visible with increasingly powerful telescopes, it became obvious that what we saw through those telescopes were stars and galaxies as they appeared a long time ago. The use of "light year" as a measurement of distance came into vogue in the 1960s, and with it the growing understanding that when modern telescopes look at objects billions of light years away, they are essentially looking backward in time. This opened up research into the history of the physical universe, as revealed by *direct astronomical observation.*

Mathematical and quantum research into the events immediately following the Big Bang merged with observational data about the formation of quasars, galaxies, stars, galaxy clusters and superclusters. These understandings, converging with our increasing understanding about the birth, development, and death of stars, gave rise to the new science of *astrophysics.*

From 1920 to the mid-1950s atomic scientists progressively developed theoretical explanations for how chemical elements could arise from the nuclear fusion dynamics within stars. After that, this field of *stellar nucleosynthesis* developed rapidly, including explanations of the observed relative abundance of the elements and their ages. It was found that each element was constructed from simpler elements and that the extreme energies of a supernova—the mega-explosion of a dying giant star—were necessary for the formation of elements heavier than iron. With these discoveries, evolutionary science gathered astronomy, physics, and chemistry together under one roof. It also became clear that planets and people—since we are made of heavier elements than hydrogen and helium—could not have come into existence before the death of prior-generation stars to provide the raw material: stardust.

Ancient red giant stars are, literally, our ancestors

So science was establishing as fact something that tribal people like Australian aborigines have believed for millennia—that the stars are our ancestors. We now know in a scientific way that we are made of stardust, a substance technically referred to as "atoms heavier than helium".

The Great Story of evolution emerged quite naturally from these understandings. It goes something like this: The Big Bang created clouds of hydrogen and helium that were drawn together into nebulae and galaxies. Concentrations of gas within galaxies collapsed through gravity and, ignited by nuclear forces, became stars. Stars, in turn, began creating elements heavier than hydrogen and helium, elements that became heavier as the star developed, with the heaviest elements created only in supernova explosions. Each supernova projected a lush smorgasbord of chemical elements millions of miles into the surrounding space. These elements, converging with other stardust through gravity—and sometimes nudged by supernova shock waves—created later-generation star systems like our solar system. Some of these included solid planets, novel objects that could only be born from the remnants of such death-exploded stars. From at least one of those stardust-built planets arose life, about whose further evolution we have learned so much and from which our kind arose.

Among our own kind, an awareness of this Great Story of evolution is spreading, along with a celebration of our place in that story, as well as evolution's ability to know itself as a fact, through us, for the first time. There is also a growing awareness that we can make a difference in the next evolutionary chapter. This is where the other parts of the Great Story get woven in—the evolution of human culture, consciousness, and technology.

The human story underwent a revolution similar to the story of the earth and the heavens. Archaeology and anthropology had been uncovering increasing insights into patterns of human cultural development, all pointing to the same kind of increasing complexity—from tribes to empires to global economies—that seemed to characterize biological and cosmic evolution.

With the industrial age the evolution of technology, too, became increasingly obvious, as technological developments built upon one another within the lifetimes of individuals, developing exponentially during the information age. The rapid development of telecommunications capacity pulled global interconnectivity and commerce with it, generating ever new social phenomena out of increasing mobility, connectivity, knowledge accessibility, distribution of authorship and power, and creative possibilities. As all this developed, human awareness—especially awareness enhanced by broadly available telecommunications and psycho-spiritual technologies—expanded and grew ever more complex.

Within biology and sociology debate raged regarding how Darwinian dynamics might apply to societies, with data growing in support of the role of "multi-level selection"—natural selection which includes selection of more successful social groups. Indeed, evolutionary biologist Richard Dawkins pointed out that culture provided a whole new medium for the exercise of Darwinian dynamics, coining the term "meme" to describe cultural patterns (ideas, behaviors, practices, images, fashions, etc.) that replicate and survive or disappear much the way genes do. Through books like *Sociobiology* and *Genes, Mind and Culture* in the 1970s and 80s, biologist and insect society authority E.O. Wilson also promoted the application of Darwinian dynamics to culture, as has Peter Richerson and Robert Boyd in their book *Not by Genes Alone*.

This inquiry into the dynamics of cultural evolution and the impact of evolutionary phenomena on our personal and social lives has extended into the 21st century. We are gaining a deepening multi-level understanding of human nature and behavior by combining the insights of brain science and evolutionary science. The evolutionary perspective clarifies not only how the more ancient parts of our brains and nervous systems influence our functioning today, but also how these factors shape—and are shaped by—relationships and cultural patterns. David Sloan Wilson's Evolution Institute offers the gifts of the evolutionary perspective to politics and governance by showing how evolutionary insights into human nature can help us formulate more effective public policy.

Within, below and above all the debate about cultural evolution, biologist Lynn Margulis and independent scientist James Lovelock argued not only that our cells evolved as synergistic communities of formerly independent bacteria and that our bodies are vast bacterial civilizations but also that the entire Earth can rightfully be regarded as a single, adaptive living organism, which they called Gaia, sustaining itself and evolving its own unprecedented systems for sustaining life. This evolved into what is now called *earth systems science* which sees life not as existing *on* a rocky planet *in* that planet's atmosphere, but rather sees it all—life, rocks, air, water, etc.—as one co-evolving whole. The most recent discoveries in this field demonstrate that rocks themselves evolve. In fact 1,250 mineral types that didn't exist prior to planets were created by

> *It turns out that rocks and cultures evolve, too, along with the rest of life*

plate tectonics and volcanoes, and 2,800 more were created by living processes over the last four billion years or so. So not only does geology bring forth biology, but biology brings forth geology. Humanity, brought forth by both, is now powerfully shaping both.

This evolving vision of a living, evolving Earth floating in a vast and evolving cosmos was epitomized in photos from space— most iconically, the image of Earth from the moon, a symbol which has had a profound impact on human consciousness.

Translating the lessons of science for spirituality, activism, and everyday life

In the mid-twentieth century a scientific evolutionary synthesis emerged in the biological sciences, placed within a broader arc of cosmological, geological, and cultural evolution by such science-integrationists as Julian Huxley (*Evolution in Action*) and Pierre Teilhard de Chardin (*The Phenomenon of Man*). This synthesis was accompanied by an emerging spiritual view of evolution, inspired by a sense of cosmic awe and belonging.

This inclusive cosmic "Great Story" or "Universe Story" spread into popular culture when Jacob Bronowski (*Ascent of Man*) and then Carl Sagan (*Cosmos*) used television as the new medium for conveying the magnificence and utility of a full-spectrum, science-based, coherent creation story.

Extending the spiritual implications (especially for traditionally religious people) of humankind's "new story" were the team of Catholic priest Thomas Berry and mathematical cosmologist Brian Swimme, culminating in their 1992 book *The Universe Story* and several video series by Swimme.

In 2006, science and culture teamed afresh in *View from the Center of the Universe* by cosmologist Joel Primack and his wife Nancy Ellen Abrams, extending mainstream evolutionary sciences artfully into the realms of meaning and value.

Meanwhile, beginning in the 1970s, the evolutionary meme was also blossoming within the human potential movement. It became a core component of the language and work of evolutionary spirituality luminaries like Deepak Chopra, Marianne Williamson, Ken Wilber, Jean Houston, Ervin László, Don Beck, Greg Braden, Duane Elgin, Joanna Macy (who promotes the idea of "deep time"), Miriam MacGillis and evolutionary enlightenment guru Andrew Cohen, as well as organizations like the Institute for Noetic Sciences and Global Mindshift, publications like *Kosmos* and the *Journal of Conscious Evolution*, and educational institutions like Wisdom University and the California Institute for Integral Studies, and more.

In the early 1980s the idea of *conscious evolution* emerged through the writings of medical researcher Jonas Salk (*Anatomy of Reality*, 1983) and psychologist Barry McWaters (*Conscious Evolution*, 1982). During the last decade, Barbara Marx Hubbard, in particular, popularized the idea (*Conscious Evolution*, 1998) and highlighted its role in the evolution of social systems and the "social potential movement". Many "conscious evolutionary leaders" like Hubbard and those in the previous paragraph took a further major step towards evolutionary activism with their 2008 "Call for Conscious Evolution",[2] declaring that "a compelling new story of our potential as a whole human species is emerging—a story of collaboration,

Conscious evolution involves awareness of the Great Story in which we are all interconnected

citizen action, dialogue and new understandings propelled by unprecedented levels of democratic freedom, multicultural exchange, and access to communication technologies. It is nothing less than the story of our collective evolution."

For many people who use the term "conscious evolution"—including most of those in the previous two paragraphs—it refers primarily to the "evolution of consciousness" in a spiritual sense, into increased awareness of the unity of all existence, which they see as the starting point for all the other kinds of change society needs. Writers like Paul Ehrlich and Robert Ornstein (*New World New Mind*), on the other hand, have used the term with no spiritual connotations at all, simply to point out that we need to take responsibility for the evolution of our culture or perish. They suggest the expansion of consciousness we need is through education and systems thinking. Both these approaches promote greater awareness of our interconnectedness. Other advocates of conscious evolution, such as "transhumanist" technological visionaries, use the phrase to refer to the creation of biological and technical alterations and enhancements of *Homo sapi-*

---

[2] care2.com/greenliving/a-call-for-conscious-evolution.html

ens to consciously create a new species far more capable than our own.

Increasingly, we find people working to pull all the stages and realms of evolution together under a single umbrella or narrative. Cosmic, stellar, geologic, biological, cultural, and technological evolution are finally being understood as aspects of one story. Historians now write about "Big History"—the history of the universe from the Big Bang onward. This cultural innovation, pioneered by Isaac Asimov and historian David Christian in the early 1990s, is now being spread by academics like Fred Spier and Cynthia Stokes Brown. Along with evolutionary scientists like Peter Corning and Eric Chaisson, these writers find that evolution's development of ever increasing complexity (undergirded, in Corning's case, by synergy) provides the coherence needed to leap across disciplines and embrace the entire 13.7 billion year story as one unbroken narrative punctuated by leaps into new realms where evolution dances in new ways.

Adding to this rich mix are recent evolutionary scientists and popularizers who see and spread applications of the evolutionary perspective (albeit mostly biological) to everyday life and social change. This burgeoning popularization ranges from David Sloan Wilson's *Evolution for Everyone* and Jonathan Haidt's *The Happiness Hypothesis* to Matt Ridley's *The Origins of Virtue* and Neil Shubin's *Your Inner Fish*.

I see as particularly relevant to this book the genre of evolutionary literature that specifically addresses the implications of evolution for societal transformation. For example, Robert Wright's *Nonzero* and John Stewart's *Evolution's Arrow* deal our need to evolve a collaborative social order; Béla Bánáthy's *Guided Evolution of Society: A Systems View* explores participatory evolutionary social systems design; Elisabet Sahtouris' *EarthDance* explores the evolutionary roots of sustainability; and Joel Garreau's *Radical Evolution* and Joel de Rosnay's *The Symbiotic Man* cover the social implications of exponential technological development.

Thus, the evolutionary meme is now not only accepted but is a ground and a frame for cultural players as diverse as academic scientists, historians, and theologians, as well as manifestations within popular culture: books, videos, and spiritual teachings. Most recently, it has ventured into personal and relationship counseling (evolutionary roots of the new turn of "positive psychology" and other forms) and into popular culture via the emergence of a whole new genre of music and music video called "Symphony of Science." We find the evolutionary perspective rapidly spreading into every niche in our cultural ecosystem.

My own engagement with the Great Story-based evolutionary worldview came from a particular branch of the conscious evolution movement: Science writer Connie Barlow, who explored the evolutionary intersection of science and spirit in her books, married long-time sustainability advocate and evolutionary evangelist Michael Dowd. For seven years they traveled together as itinerant evangelists for the Great Story of evolution, culminating in the publication of Dowd's breakthrough work *Thank God for Evolution*. From their work I experienced the evolutionary epiphany described in the Prologue of this book. My current work on evolutionary activism arises from the generative dance between Dowd's celebratory approach and my own activist perspective.

My search for evolutionary guidance for social change differs from earlier efforts like "social Darwinism" in that it assumes:

   a. Evolutionary insights—and the guidances we derive from them—will themselves evolve
   b. Cultural evolution is an emergent phenomenon arising from the interaction of diverse entities, not a program dictated by socially intelligent designers.

To be realistic, our efforts to bring consciousness—awareness, intelligence, and choice—to the evolutionary process need to proceed with abundant humility, intuition, and heart. Compared to the evolutionary process itself, we are seriously new at this and have a tremendous amount to learn.

Still, the evolutionary perspective speaks clearly to our current collective predicaments and opportunities. Indeed, it calls us to a common project—the conscious co-evolution of our social systems, technologies, cultures and consciousness.

I offer this book as a response to that call.

Since the Big Bang Never Stopped...

We are all big bang beings
breathing big bang air
on our big bang planet
as we go about our big bang business

as if it were just another day
of lonely busy self-interested selves
instead of the inexplicable Mystery
awakening together in this
Awesome Evolutionary Adventure
that we are and do.

We are both mission and banner
flapping in our cosmic dream breeze
of What Comes Next—
on fire, shape-shifting,
alive,
asleep,
turning over,
thirsty,

waking...

| ✳ |

Chapter Two

The Big CPU

I have my personal ways of thinking about and experiencing the sacredness of the evolutionary process. It is so natural to me by now that I didn't even realize, when I was putting this book together, that people might not understand a phrase like "the Creative Power of the Universe." My partner Karen Mercer suggested I say something about it early in the book. So here it is. Most of this piece came to me in an effortless flood, perhaps with some help from the CPU it describes...

Evolution is, above all, a creative undertaking. Its hallmark is novelty, but novelty is only the beginning. Novelty arises from and feeds a vast creative enterprise that never stops, a creative act we call the universe, a story being written by itself, always in search of what works, what's next, what's interesting, what's possible now.

On close examination, the whole of reality is profoundly creative, in every corner, at every scale.

The long haul of evolution seems to have started with an explosive everything-out-of-nothing event, creative to the max. Then came atoms, galaxies, stars, molecules, planets, swarms of life forms, tribes, villages, empires, opera, printing presses, global corporations, and finally skateboards, YouTube, Wikipedia, maglev trains and stick-on photovoltaic film.

Of course, something as simple as water is amazing, all by itself, when you stop to think about it. Oxygen plus hydrogen add up to this clear liquid and snow? Where does *that* come from?!!

Such miracles—most of them embraced by the new scientific meaning of "emergence"—show up everywhere. Most things have significantly different qualities than the qualities of their parts. So much novelty emerges just because of how things are arranged, or by how they happen to interact. Your body-mind is a notable example, and it's mostly made of that other miracle, water, which is itself made of ancient stardust. When we start to let this kind of thing into our awareness, the world doesn't look like the same hum-drum place anymore.

And it doesn't stop there. All this visible creative drama plays out on top of, alongside and within the normally invisible re-creation of everything that goes on all the time, happening at the quantum level, through molecular recombination, amidst ecosystem cycles like us breathing the air the trees breathed, changing it as we do. And meanwhile the Sun stirs everything around us into motion and its fellow stars keep churning out new molecules way off in their own communities light years away. This symphony of creativity is virtually infinite in its scope, depth, and complexity. And it doesn't stop.

A major quality of this symphony is that it is co-creative, co-evolutionary. Any particular thing exists because of so many other things. Events and phenomena come into being alongside one another, arising from the same ground, interacting as they go. I am because you are, and because we are, and because we are in all this together. Indeed, we are all in this together.

When I sense into this miracle of co-unfolding, it feels like something is causing it. I feel a bit like Newton under his fabled apple tree or the sunrise after Copernicus. Before Newton, things just fell. After Newton, we decided that gravity caused it, that gravity pulled the earth and the apple together. Before Copernicus, we could comfortably watch the sun rise. After Copernicus, we started sensing the world turning, while the Sun sat more or less still, a great distance away. The Beatles sang, "The fool on the hill sees the Sun going down, but the eyes in his head see the world spinning round." And this fool on the hill sees things just happening, but the eyes in his head see a great creative power at work.

While some like to put this creative power outside of reality and personalize it as The Creator, I find it more meaningful and enriching to sense the creative power as present within all aspects of Creation itself. It is a natural property of reality. The universe is fundamentally creative. Creation is what it does.

So I call this ultimate cause of everything the Creative Power of the Universe. CPU for short. (Until a second after the term came to me, I didn't think that CPU also refers to the central processing unit of a computer, the part that performs the actions for which the computer was made. In instant retrospect, I loved the "coincidence", and use it now with delight.)

Each of us is a personal expression of and channel for the Creative Power of the Universe

The Creative Power of the Universe is the Power that made the universe and remakes it every nanosecond. That doesn't mean it's off in the heavens doing its work. Sure, it's up in the heavens—and so are we!—but it is also "down here" on this planet, alive inside every problem, every crisis, every dream and possibility, every longing and epiphany.

In fact, the Creative Power of the Universe is as personal as it gets.

If we get serious about it and look carefully, we discover that CPU is inside every one of us, and we are each and all an integral part of it. It is in you as you read this, and it is in me as I write it. It is in every one of the people in your neighborhood, in your workplace, in your religious or spiritual group, your political group, your clubs and associations. It is in the folks on the other side of your email and computer game, and it is also in the people in the background and foreground of every bit of news you've ever read, seen or heard. It is in the peasant farmer, the industrial worker, the computer programmer and the stockbroker. It is in the mothers, the infants, the teenagers, the kids on their bikes and the old folks, in folks in their wheelchairs, as well as in everyone on the bus, the train, and the single-occupancy vehicles at rush hour, pushing their brakes and horns or peacefully following their breaths or tapping to the music.

There is no one outside of the Creative Power of the Universe, no one who is not participating in its Great Work.

But hardly anyone knows it. It is a big secret that you and I and everyone else are intimately connected to the most powerful and ubiquitous Power in the universe, the one that makes stars, salamanders and socialites billions of times every day, and makes them do the remarkable things they do.

Interestingly, the main thing that keeps us from becoming a conscious, powerful part of that mighty Creative Power is the assumption that we're not. That we're just little people with too much to do and not enough money or time or fun. That we're all alone trying to figure it all out ... and what's for dinner?

As evolutionary activists we can step out of that assumption and into the awareness that we are part of the ongoing creation of the universe, that our power is the Creative Power of the Universe working through us, and that we have a creative job to do, a really important undertaking to be part of. We are the eyes and ears and hands and feet and heart and mind of the Creative Power of the Universe at work in our world at this time forming the first sustainable self-evolving, wise civilization ever seen on this planet. Every decision we make—including how to spend this precious moment and where to put our precious energy and which precious people to work with and how we are going to be with them—all these decisions are the Big CPU feeling its way about what to do next here, what is possible now.

We are part of the current in the greatest river there is, the creative flow of evolution. Many of us make up that current, and we are acting together whether we know it or not. Every rush and eddy is us co-creating the flow. We don't know where it is going, but it knows, with the gravity-knowledge that all rivers possess, and we are contributing to its motion. What's more, we are learning how to do that with awareness, feeling deeply into ourselves and our world where the current is strong or stuck, tapping into the dreams of the Whole and calling them into reality, drawing them into the flow.

The rest of this book is one view of how we might go about doing all that. It comes straight from the Creative Power of the Universe and re-enters it through you. These words are the Creative Power of the Universe exploring options with itself. You and I are that Power, in that Power, of that Power.

Welcome home. We're all in this job together, backed up by the greatest creative force on Earth—and beyond.

Let's get to work, as consciously, in tune, and together as we can manage.

The Same Golden Force

The same golden force
   that drives the stars
   drives my life.
The same course of story
   beginning with
   a universe-burgeoning Bang
blesses every cell, every
   moment, every encounter,
   rich, poor, bliss, catastrophe.
Every where is the Creator
   of, by, and for all beings,
   hidden in every crevice and peak.

And today it calls me
   from inside and out
   to cease me-ing for a moment
   and see.
For alive currents divide
   along the topology of time
   and the riverflow story
is finding a line
   where we become greater than we are
   or vanish in a swansong of stardust.

For the story isn't about us.
  It is about itself—
  the wholeness of riverflow voices
of every world unflolding.
  Our choice, whatever it is,
  is part of this great story.

The Golden Explosion
  within which it all began
  is here with me now—
with in us all—longing
  with every tomorrows' child—
  holy, rising, longing to see
if we will see
  enough to be
  the next page turning
awake and golden.

| ✳ |

Reflections on

Evolutionary Activism

Chapter Three

What is the evolutionary
activist worldview?

We now know from science that everything in and around us is made of the initial Great Radiance[3] with which the universe began. There is nothing outside of that expanding exploration of creative power.

We know that all the hydrogen atoms in the water and carbohydrates in and around us are almost as old as the universe itself—13,700,000,000 years. The carbon, nitrogen and oxygen atoms that form the rest of us—and all life on Earth—

---

[3] The term "Big Bang" is the popular name for this, and is the one most often used in this book. However, the term "Great Radiance" (originated by the great CPU via Philemon Sturges) has been adopted by many spiritual evolutionaries, both for its obvious spiritual connotations and for the fact that it is more exact: There was no "bang" at the beginning because there was no medium for sound.

came into being in the bellies of red giant stars that lived and died before our sun was born. The more complex elements—calcium and magnesium, gold and silver, and all the rest—were created in supernova explosions brighter than a billion stars, flung to the far ends of the galaxy as raw materials for Life.

It is not mysticism but hard science that now tells us we are made of stardust and light, waves and coalescences of stardust and light reconfiguring into cars and trees, oceans and civilizations. We are cosmic evolution, happening right here and now. We are the living face of evolution, the eyes and hands and minds of the universe weaving itself into its next manifestations, day after day after day. We are the universe becoming conscious, watching itself through microscopes and telescopes, mountaintops and meditations, awed, nudging its pieces into greater awareness and love.

We are both the universe's sleep and the universe's awakening

We are also the universe broken apart in the illusion of separateness, the arrogance of our small but growing power, the pursuit of our small but growing desires. And we are the universe waking up from this dream of separateness and smallness into the discovery of ourselves as conscious, loving Evolution, finding ever more remarkable and inclusive forms of cooperation. We are both the universe's sleep and the universe's awakening.

Here on Earth we are stardust-as-human-civilization, dawning into an evolutionary imperative: the creation of a collectively wise culture that is capable of its own conscious evolution. This unprecedented challenge is more than an enticing possibility. It is a collective necessity, a matter of survival. It *is* our next evolutionary leap and we *are* that leap.

And to take this collective evolutionary step, evolutionary activism is crucial. The values, impulses, and determination of evolutionary activists—of evolution*aries*—are the essential creative trajectory of evolution itself surging into its next unprecedented form, pushing through us into reality. There is no boundary, no distinction between this vast and ancient creative Intelligence and ourselves. It is everything we are, everything we do.

It is the wind in our sails. And if we look closely enough, we will see that we are that wind, we are those sails... We are the stars and the sky and the sea and the storm-tasting weave of the Journey that is every journey that ever was, surging into now...

Showing Up

We are the world
  showing up as a body.

We are universal consciousness
  showing up as one mind.

We are everything
  showing up as one thing.

We are the essence of humanity
  showing up as diverse people.

We are interconnectedness itself
  showing up as separate selves.

We are every generation
  showing up as our generation.

We are aliveness
  showing up as alive.

We are the end
  showing up as the beginning
  and the beginning
  as the end

    and the story
    as it writes Itself...

| ✳ |

Chapter Four

My evolution into evolutionary activism

My activism has been unfolding in layers for more than five decades. Below is the story of that evolution through an expanding series of inquiries in which each question has embraced, responded to, and reverberated beyond the previous one, like a set of concentric circles rippling out over the pond of my life into the larger world.

I began as a child activist in a progressive activist family in the 1950s. Given the unprecedented threat of global nuclear holocaust during the Cold War, my early activism was focused in the peace movement and action for nuclear disarmament. Since then, I have kept my activist orientation, but transformed it continually, grounded in a profound question that many of us share:

How can I help make a better world?

This core question lives in a white heat at the center of my life, informing everything I think and do. But it was only a beginning. It led me to the Great Peace March of 1986, the watershed event of my life, which triggered a cascade of compelling inquiries that shaped the evolution of my activism over the next 23 years. I wondered:

1. What is the meaning of the self-organized COLLECTIVE INTELLIGENCE I experienced on the Great Peace March?

Two weeks after its launch, the march lost its leadership, resources, and 800 marchers. The remaining 400 marchers reorganized with no top-down leadership and managed to make our way across the US in 9 months with no major snafus. How? What was the big lesson here? Exploring this in the early 1990s led me to the idea of *co-intelligence*, which includes collective intelligence, non-rational intelligences, collaborative intelligence, universal intelligence, and more. Intelligence helps us succeed and I was seeking a fuller form of intelligence that would answer this question:

2. How can the ACTIVIST GROUPS I support become more collaboratively effective?

Such groups are, ironically, notoriously fractious. Exploring this question led me to a whole world of methodologies for effective group work and organizational revitalization. The more I learned, the more I realized that radically different people *could* work together well. Ironically, that insight ultimately dissolved my progressive perspective, for I realized that even liberals and conservatives could and should work together. My inquiry expanded beyond helping activist groups, into this question:

3. How can COMMUNITIES and COUNTRIES be more collaboratively effective?

My explorations thus led me to try weaving diverse methodologies into a coherent whole, seeing how they complemented one another and together implied a radically different form of society. I began to envision a "wise democracy" and the kind of institutions that would serve it. Realizing how many of those institutions already existed as prototypes around the world led me to write my book *The Tao of Democracy* in 2003. Also, between 1998 and 2005 I explored the transformative potential of crises like climate change, 9-11 and Y2K to instigate such a wise democracy, leading to my next inquiry:

How can we create a wise democracy out of crisis?

4. How can humanity wisely and creatively work with the CRISES of our time?

We face unprecedented challenges, mostly of our own making. They are becoming increasingly obvious in our everyday lives, bringing fear, uncertainty, and opportunity. Dealing with them well will involve transforming our world and ourselves. The wise democracy vision offered both an inspiring goal and powerful activist tools. Michael Dowd, one of my colleagues in using the Y2K crisis to further sustainability, asked me to help him organize the first Evolutionary Salon in 2005. This remarkable experience evoked two new questions that were soon shifting the meaning of everything I was doing:

5. How can we help our social systems and cultures CONSCIOUSLY EVOLVE?

Increasingly I saw democracy and activism as means through which societies learn and nonviolently transform themselves. I realized our task as activists is not so much solving problems or building utopia, as becoming wise agents of transformation—conscious participants in the ongoing evolution of consciousness, culture, and social systems. The first Evolutionary Salon envisioned "a movement for the conscious evolution of increasingly conscious social systems." Soon thereafter I had an evolutionary epiphany (described in the prologue of this book) that turned all this inside-out into an even more profound and meaningful question...

6. How can we grow into BEING EVOLUTION—and taking responsibility for our role *as* the increasingly conscious co-intelligence of the universe?

I sensed a shift in which I ceased being a conscious participant in the evolutionary process and became the process itself. Suddenly, *my* story stretched back 14 billion years and every moment became a sacred opportunity for more conscious action. I found myself being a finger of the cosmic Hand, a wave of its Ocean, a synapse of its Mind.

And so, while this seems to be the story of how one "change agent"—me—evolved, it is actually part of a larger story of how evolution itself is becoming conscious on Earth right here and now. An activism which studies evolutionary dynamics that can be used to develop increasingly conscious social systems is an activism that is one part of the process of evolution itself, evolving—waking up into doing things consciously that it has done unconsciously for billions of years.

All my previous world-betterment, co-intelligence and wise democracy work has been part of that. Seeing my work as creating increasingly conscious social systems puts it into a larger context and suggests a source of guidance for the future—evolution itself.

Seeing evolution, being evolution, also moves me—and us, as activists—beyond issues and solutions. This stance offers a new story about what change is, who we are, and what we are doing here. So:

> *How do we activists humbly BECOME the world consciously evolving in directions that deeply support all forms of aliveness?*

I see that as the inquiry at the very heart of evolutionary activism.

A Prayer of Evolutionary Affirmation

... My life is a gift
from the whole of Life
to the whole of Life...

That emergent part of my life
that I think of as "me"
gets to evolve
by practicing stewardship of my life
within and as—and in service to—
the sacred Web of Life
within and as—and in service to—
the great sacred Story
of our self-spinning Universe
whose weave and tale we follow
and are.

May I be this Flow.
May I be this Yes.
May it be so.

| ✳ |

Chapter Five

What is evolutionary activism?

I see evolutionary activism as social change work

a. *inspired* by the story of evolution and the fact that we are the process of evolution becoming conscious of itself;
b. *guided* in its rationale, strategies, and tactics by evolutionary dynamics rather than any other political ideology or agenda; and
c. *focused* on altering the causal stories, structures and systems of society—the social DNA—so that society develops and reproduces in more healthy ways, moving beyond patterns that have proven unsustainable toward patterns that serve life more broadly and deeply.

Evolutionary activists continually seek to more deeply understand evolutionary dynamics—from cosmic to biological to cultural to personal—in order to embody and use those dynamics to further the vibrancy and creative adaptability of the living systems they are part of.

Evolutionary activists know they are part of a 13.7 billion year old story of Creative Radiance and stardust reconfiguring into ever more remarkable ways to be whole—and that this sacred storm is unfolding now, through and as themselves and their world, in the realms of consciousness and civilization, from which they are not separate.

Evolutionary activists are acutely aware that their learning about evolutionary dynamics, and their application of those understandings to the life and systems in, among and around them *are* evolution becoming conscious of itself. The seriousness and playfulness with which they pursue this *is* the evolutionary impulse through which the world deepens, complexifies and transforms itself.

Beyond "becoming the change they seek", evolutionary activists become aware of actually being the process of change itself.

Other dimensions and forms of evolutionarily significant behavior

There are many related phenomena that exist in and outside of the world of explicitly evolutionary activism. Getting clear on them can help clarify what evolutionary activism, itself, is. Definitions for some of these phenomena are offered here, providing language that validates while distinguishing them from the main subject of this book.

Evolutionary participation: Our role in evolution. Everything we do plays a role in evolution. We *are* participants in evolution, whether we know it or not, whether we want to be or not.

We play a role in evolution, no matter what we do

Evolutionary awareness: Awareness that evolution is happening now; that it is happening in, among and around us; that it is happening not only in nature (and our impacts on the natural world) and through genetic engineering but in and through culture, social systems, technologies, and all other aspects of our humanity; that it is reshaping our lives and our world in profound ways; and that we are playing a role in how it unfolds, no matter what we do. The greater someone's evolutionary awareness, the more of these processes they perceive and the deeper their understanding of each one.

Conscious evolutionary action: Playing our evolutionary role consciously and choicefully. Conscious participation can be pursued at any scale, from individual to universal.

Evolutionary leadership: Taking initiative to increase evolutionary consciousness in individuals and collectives and to further the evolutionary leaps humanity needs at this time.

Evolutionary agentry: Being a conscious, willing, intentional instrument or agent of the creative process of evolution. Such agentry can be guided by calling and inspiration and/or by what we can learn of the dynamics of evolution, how evolution does what it does, so we can do that consciously and with whatever wisdom we can muster.

*NOTE: Evolutionary activism could be defined as serious evolutionary action, agentry, or leadership **that is engaged in transforming social systems**.*

Evolutionary impact: Any influence on evolutionary consciousness and/or evolutionary leaps, with or without intending that effect or undertaking such activity in connection with the evolutionary story. Some change agents and "non-evolutionary" activists have significant evolutionary impact without necessarily knowing it. The term "impact" here is intended to connote something more consequential than the inevitable "evolutionary participation" in which we are all involved. Examples are the development of sustainable technologies and the convening of powerful conversations, even when they are initiated by people without explicit evolutionary awareness.

Evolutionary artistry: Evolutionary agentry or activism at the edge of emergence and consciousness, which is characterized by elegant, mindful intelligence, "skillful means", creativity and an aesthetic that moves towards beauty, simplicity, and life energy and away from force and waste. It efficiently and elegantly catalyzes the life energies of the systems and situations it engages towards healthy transformation, often with story, the arts, spirit, and conversation.

Evolutionary flow: Conscious evolutionary activity that pervades one's whole life, of which one's self is but a facet. Beyond being an evolutionary *agent*, one lives in and as the evolutionary impulse, disappearing as a separate entity and manifesting as one aspect of the creative energy implicit in— and driving—the unfolding process of evolution. This is comparable to other flow phenomena, which often have a spiritual dimension. "Flow" was first popularized by Mihaly Csikszentmihalyi in his 1988 book *Optimal Experience: Psychological Studies of Flow in Consciousness,* describing the dissolution of participants' sense of a separate self in the seamless flow of teamwork in sports and improvisational jazz ensembles "in the groove". It is characterized by appropriate action with little if any forethought, arising from the whole, with participants acting smoothly as part of the whole as fingers act fluidly as parts of the hand. Thus "flow".

Riotous Meadow People

We're a meadow, not a highway,
a process, not a plan.
The space we make helps people take
their futures in their hands
to sow the world with selves and dreams
to blossom once again.

It's not a single dream we sow,
nor even garden rows —
the meadow reaches everywhere
and riotously grows,
a passionate diversity
no one designer chose.

Our meadow happens naturally,
It fills a space left bare.
Yet still we must protect it,
admire it and care
enough about tomorrow
to have a meadow there.

| ✳ |

Chapter Six

What makes evolutionary activism different from other forms of activism?

Evolutionary activism, as I see it at this stage, is distinguished by one or more of the following characteristics. The more of these interrelated qualities we find in any particular change effort, the more valid and clarifying I think the label "evolutionary" would be in referring to it. Perhaps more importantly, these qualities, taken together, vividly paint the vision of a social change movement that seems to be seeking expression (at least through me) at this time. Lastly, all these principles of evolutionary activism apply, quite naturally, to evolutionary leadership, as well.

1. Evolutionary activism promotes healthy self-organization and the conscious evolvability of whole systems.

Evolutionary activists and leaders share an assumption that the most important information, energy and resources a human system (from an individual to a society) needs for its transformation is already present in the system, awaiting proper designs, invitations, and interactions to do their transformational work. So evolutionary activists and leaders engage diverse parts of a target system—as well as related systems around it—in the work of collective self-organization and mutual transformation.

Most evolutionary activists and leaders work in some way with nonlinear dynamics—feedback loops, energy fields, intuitive longings, stories and images, etc.—that enable systems to sustain and transform themselves in concert with shifting internal and external realities. They focus on things like sustainability, knowledge systems, collective intelligence and wisdom, cultural stories, economic indicators, interconnectivity, and so on. They recognize the importance of intention, design, and other initial conditions—as well as ongoing structures, patterns, and technologies of interaction—in the functioning of complex living systems.

Evolutionary activists work with nonlinear dynamics and emergence

Some evolutionary activists and leaders use maps of human development to create social and psycho-spiritual spaces for the flourishing of diverse developmental stages, and for the progress of people and cultures from one stage to another. Other evolutionary leaders and activists focus on the dynamics of emergence that enable human systems to discover and move into their next as-yet-unknown pattern of function-ality and wholeness.

As holistic, multi-level systems thinkers, many evolu-tionary activists and leaders develop their capacity to see systems, to understand their role in the whole, to observe their own interactions, and to comprehend the larger struc-tures, norms, processes, technologies, beliefs and stories that influence their lives and the lives of whole systems. They learn to work with these as both objects and allies.

And they understand and work with the intimate inter-relationship between individual and collective dynamics, between consciousness and social systems, and between mind, body, spirit, and other dimensions of our full humanity. For we are whole beings, embedded in dynamic wholeness.

2. Evolutionary activism uses strategic questions and stra-tegic conversations as primary transformational modes.

"Strategic" here means questions and conversations that are designed to release transformational energy in specific situations where evolutionary activists or leaders believe such energy is clearly needed, stuck, trying to emerge, or seeking creative outlets. Powerful questions create a bounded, ener-gized space—a new territory that invokes passionate explo-ration—where new insights and possibilities can arise from what has heart and meaning for the people involved. Pow-erful conversations based on such questions carry people, consciousness, and whole systems from wherever they happen to be into new states with greater potential, alive-ness, and functionality.

Since the Big Bang, *interaction* has been the driving force of evolution. For the evolution of human consciousness and social systems, high quality interactive conversation offers the most evolutionary benefit at the least cost. So evolutionary activists and leaders not only convene strategic conversations, but play an active role in the innovative flowering of power-ful forms of conversation that support whole-system change and collective intelligence.

3. Evolutionary activism engages diversity and dissonance creatively in the service of greater life.

Dissonance includes disagreement, problems, crises, pain, upset, frustration, destruction, and all forms of distur-bance—including positive disturbances such as innovation, vision, insight, inspiration, longing, etc. Dissonance includes anything that interrupts or impedes business as usual, thereby opening space for potentially valuable novelty to emerge.

Evolutionary activists and leaders understand that evolu-tion involves a dance between dissonance and coherence. Life finds something that works (a coherence) until internal or exter-nal changes disturb it (dissonance), calling forth new structures, actions, cultures, etc.—which then constitute a new *fit* within a new environment (i.e., a new coherence). More often than not, change or novelty in one area disturbs something some-where else, and the evolutionary dance proceeds...

Much of evolutionary activism involves nothing more than *conscious engagement in this dance.* Thus the focus on in-cluding diversity, welcoming voices from the fringe, seeing opportunity in crises, and attending to the gifts hidden in the disturbances of our individual and collective lives. And thus our humility regarding what we know and do, and the lightness with which we hold our work (even in the midst of passion), our patience with "the unknown" and our ultimate respect for the creative power of Mystery: for whatever we know will someday be yesterday's knowledge, and whatever forms we establish will one day pass away.

Evolutionary activism taps the gifts of disturbance to move the situation toward positive possibility

4. Evolutionary activism highlights, uses, and promotes the energy of positive possibility.

Possibilities are not just vague narratives. They exist in and arise from real people and real situations. They have resonance and energy. When recognized and supported, they call us into real-izing them (making them real) among us. Evolutionary activists and evolutionary leaders use this fact as a resource for positive transformation.

In doing so, most evolutionary activists maintain a fundamentally appreciative stance in their work. Appreciation clearly sees what is, notices and values the positive dimensions of it or in it, and then validates and adds value and power to those positive dimensions. This is not a matter of ignoring problems or the darker dimensions of reality. It is a matter of empowering the capacity of life energy to find its way towards new forms of coherence and wellbeing—a capacity for healing, transformation and Grace that is intrinsic to Life. Many evolutionary practices explicitly tap into and/or follow existing and emerging life energies present in every situation.

These positive energies show up in struggling institutions, in challenged communities, and in individual vocations and avocations where a person's gifts and passions meet the world's needs. There is evolutionary artistry in appreciating and welcoming the perfect fit between the emerging energies and what the situation warrants, rather than imposing our own sense of what should happen. It is like sensitively sailing the winds of change rather than determinedly motoring through the waves against the current. At its best, the activist or leader becomes one with the emerging change in that effortlessly elegant state known as "flow," thereby *becoming* the work of evolution itself.

5. Evolutionary activism consciously seeks and uses guidance from evolutionary dynamics.

Evolution is the mother of all change processes. With 13.7 billion years of experience, evolution has developed deep and expansive wisdom about functionality and change in complex systems. Evolutionary leaders and activists see evolution and natural systems as their primary teachers and take the trouble to study them.

While acknowledging differences in the dynamics of cosmic, stellar, geologic, chemical, biologic, and cultural evolution, evolutionary activists and leaders also know these have many patterns in common. They feel challenged both to apply evolutionary understandings appropriately and to create new evolutionary dynamics appropriate to the current situation. As students they learn from the Masters—and then innovate.

They see value, for example, in such evolutionary dynamics as nurturing and connecting diverse prototypes and pilot projects in diverse areas—creating interactive ecosystems of evolutionary innovation and learning communities of evolutionary innovators—a practice which mimics the creative role of genetic diversity in natural selection.

They seek ways to align the self-interests of individuals, corporations and societies with the wellbeing of the whole human and natural systems they are part of—an alignment that has occurred in the formation of every complex system that has survived in the past.

They understand today's challenge to be the creation of a global meta-organism from diverse individuals, groups, organizations, communities, networks, and nations—which is not unlike the challenge faced by independent cells in forming multicellular organisms millions of years ago. Evolutionary activists know that this will require creative transformation of competitive and cooperative dynamics to embody the reality that we are all in this (and need to evolve) together.

These are but a few insights offered by evolution to guide evolutionary activists and leaders, who make it a practice to study evolution to more deeply understand how it works and how to live it consciously in today's world.

6. Evolutionary activism considers co-creativity the sacred essence and power of its work.

Evolution is not just creative at every level of existence; it is co-creative, always involving in-

*How can the
dance of
diverse
self-interests
be engaged
in service to
the whole?*

teractions among diverse entities to generate new phenomena. This co-creativity is intrinsic to reality, to life: nothing happens without it. We cannot escape the fact that we are co-creative participants in all that happens. Our challenge is not to participate and get others to do so, for we are all already participating to the max. Our challenge is to become more conscious and wise in our evolutionary participation and co-creativity.

Thus there is little blame, shame, guilt or regret—nor even pride—in conscious evolutionary agentry, for evolutionary activists and leaders realize there are no single causes and no lone agents. Indeed, they may even celebrate people and institutions who play significant roles in generating the dangerous imbalances that will in turn provoke life-serving, life-saving responses from significant others or the general public; in other words, they may appreciate the very people and institutions attacked by their more traditional activist colleagues or seen as problems by traditional leaders.

More pro-actively, evolutionary activists and leaders may exercise a strategic creativity intended and designed to evoke the life-affirming co-creative engagement of others, as the classic nonviolent movements of Gandhi and King engaged the public and power-holders in transformation through their well-publicized civil disobedience.

Such activism and leadership can have a cosmic dimension, as well. Some spiritually oriented evolutionary activists and leaders see God as the co-creative Power of the universe, and so may see their own work as a vibrant and spiritually significant manifestation of God's Power here and now—through them and those they engage—in the ongoing transformation of our world. Again, this is parallel to the nonviolent activists like Gandhi and King who believe their success lies in the transformative power of Truth and Love that they experience as coming from God.

7. Evolutionary activism sees itself as part of the Great Story of Evolution becoming conscious of itself, and invites others into that story.

The factual story of evolution provides a profoundly meaningful context for whatever actions we do on Earth today. This is even more true for evolutionary activists and leaders seeking to participate in evolution consciously or to *be* evolution. As part of that story, their work has a mythic heroic quality, although manifesting in a more humble, catalytic, co-creative way than we normally associate with "heroes" and "leaders."

Evolutionary activists and leaders know that their power is not theirs, but is the creative power of evolution itself—as old as the universe, as wise as nature. They are but stewards and channels for that immense and ancient power, opening themselves to the unfolding story in, through, and around them. This story is so meaningful, liberating, and empowering to them that they seek to share it with others.

In a more pro-active sense, many evolutionary activists and leaders frame their role as bringing greater consciousness—greater attention, awareness, understanding, intelligence, wisdom, compassion, and choice—to the co-evolutionary process in human affairs, in both its individual and collective manifestations. As part of evolution becoming more conscious, they look for, support, and use educational and conversational opportunities, cultural stories, social systems, spiritual practices, art and performance, and other means to transcend the current constraints on human awareness and wise engagement in evolving a better world together.

This 21st century vision of evolutionary activism seeks to reclaim the word "activist" from its 20th century connotations of militancy, of adversarial positions and battles over issues and candidates. "Activism" can mean simply our active engagement to co-create a better future by changing dysfunctional social conditions and social systems. All forms of activism do that and—like all forms of human life—participate in the unfolding drama of evolution. This chapter describes the trademark ways evolutionary activism has of doing that.

Star Story Children

We come from fire
    from fire and silence.
We are embers of stars,
    embers of stellar explosions,
    embers of the biggest bang being ever
    glowing and fading,
    glowing again, fading brightly
    making one whole slow motion explosion
    over spacing reaches of time
    and timelessness
    of mind and story
we are
    green with new energy,
    red and breathing with shine
    and void and silence
    our voice, our eon yawn crying
    cloudy with suns and stars
    long in the turning,
    spiraling our way in the slow
    living burn of tomorrow,
    the slow living turn of tomorrow
the slow
    living fire of the high
    sky grounding
Who We Are.

| ✳ |

Chapter Seven

Learning to *be* evolution

*If we wish to consciously evolve as a civilization,
evolution has some lessons we need to start learning,
taking seriously, and applying.*

First of all, I want to be clear that "learning to *be* evolution" is
not about Darwin or genetic engineering. It is bigger than
that, much bigger. Those pursuing this inquiry see Charles
Darwin as a genius who opened new realms of understanding, while at the same time provoking profoundly deeper
questions about what's really happening in evolutionary
processes. Furthermore, we are exploring not only the evolution of living species, but the evolution of the cosmos, the
planet, society—everything from natural laws to the shape of
our everyday lives.

Evolution is the process of change—ongoing transformational change. It is the cumulative development of life, unfolding slowly and incrementally, with occasional sudden bursts of creativity and novelty, with evolutionary opportunities sprouting in climates of crisis. We are living through one of these disorienting bursts of creativity and crisis right now.

Through evolution new forms appear—new organisms, new partnerships, new conditions, new systems. Some of them last and some don't. Evolution tests things out. Evolutionary testing goes on at every level, all the time. The universe does it. Life does it. Human societies do it. You and I are doing it every day—sometimes in our lives, sometimes in our minds, sometimes in our conversations. New patterns rise and fall.

Billions of years of creative trial and error have added up to the world we live in. Some of that world is profoundly exciting and enjoyable. Some of it is increasingly scary. Things are getting better and better and worse and worse, faster and faster. Much of it is changing faster than we can follow—novelty and complexity racing ahead of our individual capacity to understand and respond.

We face daunting choices about how to respond to changes that seem forced upon us. We also face compelling choices about creating a better world from the depths of our hearts and our dreams.

How did we end up in this place? Individually and collectively, we are products of evolution. Evolution produced us through 13.7 billion years of trial and error and gradually increasing awareness and responsiveness, culminating in a few thousand years of more or less conscious choices by thousands of people we call our parents, leaders, elders, ancestors. They foresaw little of what life would be like right now.

And now *we* are the ones making choices that are shaping the evolution of the future—not only future generations of humanity but future generations of all life on Earth.

How conscious are we about who we are, what we are doing, where our motivations come from, and the consequences of the choices we make? Do we realize that our awareness, our intelligence, our desires and dreams, our creativity and efforts—seasoned by wisdom, or not—have *become* evolution, right here on Earth, at least for now?

We are half-blind, half-awake, less than half wise

Nothing on Earth can compete with the impact of 21st century humanity. Collectively we have become a semi-conscious branch of evolution. We are the shapers of the ongoing processes of transformational change—half blind, half awake, less than half wise.

It is slowly dawning on us that our species will flourish or fade away, owing to the evolutionary choices we make now, whether or not we know what we are doing.

We are at a critical stage in our remarkable human journey on this planet: We are coming to a place where the road ends. From here on out, we will be making the road as we walk it, in ways we've never had to do before. We now have the job of forging our own evolutionary destiny, and being prime agents of the process of evolution here on Earth. It behooves us to learn something about the job description.

Learning *from* evolution how to *be* evolution

Lessons from our long evolutionary journey offer rich sources of guidance about how to consciously participate in the evolutionary process. Taking this guidance on "evolutionary participation" seriously can help us transform ourselves, our consciousness, our social systems and cultures, and our technologies in ways that serve our long-term collective flourishing as part of a flourishing Earth.

Listed below are just a few of the evolutionary dynamics and opportunities we can explore and use. Each is described further at the end of this chapter. (Original research by Peggy Holman and myself in 2007 was supported by a grant from the W. K. Kellogg Foundation.) A major project of the Co-Intelligence Institute now is identifying and understanding more of such dynamics and how best to apply them all, and spreading that new, ancient knowledge.

1. **CREATIVE USE OF DISTURBANCE.** A major driver of evolution is creative response to challenges, diversity, conflict, crisis and disturbances of all kinds. Our uniqueness— our individual specialness—and the unique challenges, tensions and possibilities of every moment—are nascent resources for the world, vast and usually overlooked or wasted. Seeing this can inspire us, in times of collective trauma, to move beyond peacemaking and crisis management to seeing possibilities and catalyzing inclusive evolutionary breakthroughs, tapping the dissonance as a source of insight and energy.

2. **A NEW DANCE OF COOPERATION AND COMPETITION.** Evolution has evolved with cooperation enhancing

competitiveness. As we become a global society, competition will necessarily evolve to support cooperation.

3.   SYNERGY BETWEEN SELF AND WHOLE. Life on Earth finds novel ways for self-interest and the whole to serve each other. We are called to create new ways to design this dynamic into complex 21st century societies.

4.   HIGHER LEARNING. Evolution is itself a vast learning enterprise, an endless process of discovery—and emergence is its learning edge. That edge involves new forms of ongoing collective intelligence and wisdom, and reframing education to meet the challenges of conscious collective evolution. By its nature, learning on the edge requires a growing capacity to embrace the unknown.

5.   SELF-ORGANIZATION AND EMERGENCE. As evolution brings forth increasing complexity from simple beginnings, it creates remarkable ways for life to self-organize without top-down direction. Our social and technological complexity is now calling forth new forms of creative, conscious human self-organization.

6.   EVOLVING CONSCIOUSNESS. From microbes swimming towards food to the global scientific community tracking climate change, evolution has been developing the capacity of life to be aware. Human consciousness shapes social systems and culture—and social systems and culture shape consciousness. This insight, combined with new and ancient methods of expanding consciousness, offer tremendous leverage for humanity's conscious evolution.

7. IT'S ABOUT PROCESS. The essence of evolution is the emergence of outcomes from powerful interactive processes. But it isn't about being attached to particular outcomes, since they, too, will change and evolve. If we want to become evolution, we would be wise to learn how to let go and focus on manifesting powerfully interactive, life-serving processes.

We live in a universe of bonded, self-organizing wholeness, waking up

8. LOVE AT THE CORE. As gravity holds us all in one embrace and our common past makes us kin, deep inside we know our connection, we feel its call. This deep truth can be called forth to help us resonate with one another. Much of what we need to do next taps into and is empowered by the powerful reality of our affiliation.

9. GRACE MOVES IT ALL. From moment to moment, we and all the rest of life are wholeness en route to its next state of wholeness. Such is the deepest urge of Life. This ongoing impetus towards wholeness is the fundamental dynamic underlying the Creative Power of the Universe which manifests in and around us as evolution. It unfolds at every level, in every moment, and everything we do is part of it. There is no higher calling than the conscious participation in Grace, the ongoing creation of wholeness.

These nine evolutionary dynamics and the evolutionary projects they point to and inspire are but a taste of the rich guidance available from the serious study of evolution's relevance for today. There are dozens of other dynamics and patterns revealed by evolutionary science and related studies which could also guide us—and new ones are being discovered every year.

We are just beginning to learn how to apply these emerging understandings to our lives, our societies, and our efforts to make a better world. This is a new field of study and practice. Its insights will help us see where our energy, attention and resources can be most usefully focused to build a more sustainable, just, and life-serving civilization.

Perhaps most remarkably, in doing this work—to the extent we learn to consciously apply the dynamics that are *already* at work in the evolution of life—we are actually becoming a manifestation of evolution in a totally new realm— *conscious evolution.*

Just as evolution shifted into major new realms of creativity when it discovered cells... then sexual reproduction... then multicellular organisms... then language... it is now shifting into a remarkable new game as it becomes conscious of itself, through us, and begins to consciously perform its transformational magic—even consciously evolving its own consciousness into more profound states.

To make crystal clear what we are dealing with here: "conscious evolution" is not primarily about the genetic engineering of individual animals, plants, and humans. It is about far greater, more productive and vital challenges—the conscious evolution of our societies, our lives, and our individual and collective consciousness—and the conscious evolution of the knowledge, arts and technologies that will make those developments possible. Therein lie tremendous hope for our civilization and an inspiring new view of who we are and what we are doing in this universe.

For we are not just organisms trying to survive, accidents of mutating materiality, or isolated individuals consuming one more wave of well-advertised products. In a very profound sense, we are the universe itself beginning another chapter in its truly remarkable, wildly creative, and keenly experimental Great Story-of-all-stories.

What we do next will be profoundly important—no matter what.

So let us take a moment to look more closely at these initial nine examples of evolutionary guidance.

1. CREATIVE USE OF DISTURBANCE. Evolution has a field day with differences, dynamic tensions, crises, indeed all forms of disturbance. Disturbance disturbs a comfortable fit, a seemingly stable status quo, instigating the emergence of Grace in search of life's next fit, its next state of wholeness. Diversity is one of the most potent sources of dissonance, a stimulant of Grace and an enricher of love. Dynamic, interacting diversity is one of the deepest and most widespread realities in the universe, an engine of evolution, source of creativity and transformational crises. Just as we all arise from stardust, we are each profoundly unique. Society can gloss over our uniqueness with conformity, prejudice, and politeness—trying to restrain our mind-boggling diversity— but diversity refuses to disappear, and it constantly struggles to show up, to be recognized, to make a difference. When our differences come vividly into view, they often disturb our simple certainties and comfortable order. Those disturbances almost always mark something new and important trying to surface in our midst, so today we need to hear the call to acknowledge our differences while remaining connected with one another. Welcoming diversity and disturbance, and engaging them creatively, are powerful conscious acts that catalyze emergence at the growing edge of evolution. Efforts to simply resolve, solve, ameliorate, and calm troubled waters can short-circuit important opportunities for transformation. Our capacitance— our individual and collective capacity to welcome, hold in dynamic tension, and creatively engage with diversity, dissonance, uncertainty, and complexity—is a hallmark of co-intelligence and a source of evolutionary energy and guidance.

> *Dynamic, interacting diversity is a powerful engine of evolution*

2.   A NEW DANCE OF COOPERATION AND COMPETITION. Those who today detect directionality in the history of life note that evolution through time has produced ever more inclusive and intricate systems of cooperation, from molecular synergies to the global financial web of Visa. Cooperative achievements have been retained by the body of life not at the expense of competition but in service to it: Quite simply, cooperating entities are usually more robust in handling the challenges offered up by the world around them and thus they beat their competition. However, this dynamic is now undergoing a radical shift. As human activities expand to embrace the global commons we all share, the win/lose games that drove human interactions in the past are being supplanted by cooperative games that recognize we are now all in it together. Our exploding power has made it clear that, in the final analysis, we will either win together or lose together. More inclusive, sophisticated forms of cooperation are no longer simply admirable; they are essential. In the next evolutionary surge, competition will be honed for its best gifts—driving creativity and excellence—but contained and constrained within globally cooperative contexts.

3.   SYNERGY BETWEEN SELF AND WHOLE. Because individual organisms play their role in biological evolution by passing on genes, self-interest is foundational in biological evolution. And yet it is evident that the evolutionary benefits of cooperation throughout the journey of life have been achieved by creatively tying self-interest to the welfare of the whole. Sustainable cooperative systems thus contain feedback loops that help individuals experience the positive and negative effects of their own acts. On that loom, individual gifts can then be woven into patterns that serve the whole even as the whole enhances the lives of its individual members. Under the right social conditions, individuals "taking responsibility for what they love" generate greater life for their whole group or society. The job of evolutionary activism is to bring about those "right social conditions."

This is evolutionary science. This is evolutionary economics. This is evolutionary sociology. This is evolutionary politics and governance.

4. HIGHER LEARNING. Evolution is a vast learning enterprise. In biological evolution, learning happens when organisms pass information from one generation to the next, using the genetic language of DNA. New genetic approaches (mutations, sexual recombinations, etc.) get tested in new environments, and workable ones spread. This change-and-test evolutionary intelligence changed radically—accelerating and freeing life from many harsh consequences—when it became embodied in minds that could test ideas and options in virtual safety before trying them out in the physical and social worlds. Then, as symbolic language emerged in the human realm, this intelligence became augmented by increasingly sophisticated methods for developing and transmitting knowledge over time and space—writing, education, printing, science, telecommunications, the internet. And with those developments, collective intelligence—which began with multicellular organisms and social insects—rapidly evolved into totally new realms. Today, increasingly inclusive forms of collective intelligence and wisdom nurture our capacitance for embracing and creatively engaging with complexity, uncertainty, and mystery at the emerging edge of evolution. Quite naturally, this rapidly evolving higher learning is beginning to explore the subject of evolution itself and, in the process, *becoming* an evolved, more self-aware form of evolution.

5. SELF-ORGANIZATION AND EMERGENCE. Evolution has steadily enriched the capacity of life to organize itself into ever-more creative, remarkable, complex, and workable forms. The wonder of the universe is not that it was designed from outside, but that it is designing itself from the inside, and getting better and better at doing so. (Some say God manifests in this intimate, imminent, infinite, ever-expanding creativity.) As complexity increases, linear forms of understanding and management become less and less workable—both in the realm

Self-organization helps us creatively engage increasing complexity

of human societies and ecologically in the world at large. The complexity sciences have vividly demonstrated that life operates primarily with distributed, evocative, loopy, self-generating, whole-system organic forms of organization and leadership, rather than through straight lines, boxes, command hierarchies, conformity, and unchanging rules (some scientists are now suggesting that even the deepest laws of nature evolve). Using whole-system forms of intelligence, life generates its own newness at the evolutionary edge, which we humans experience as emergence, as a creative upwelling within us, among us and around us. The growing body of knowledge about healthy self-organization and emergence can help us transform problems and crises into evolutionary leaps.

6.　EVOLVING CONSCIOUSNESS. Most native peoples experience the world as alive and aware: stones, mountains, forests, plants, animals are all alive and conscious, each in their own ways. Drawing upon mainstream science, as well as these indigenous roots, many other people are beginning to recover similar forms of depth communion with the more-than-human world. The resulting deep sense of interconnectedness engenders a more sensitive relationship with nature. In addition, for thousands of years, pioneers committed to exploring the interior dimension of reality have explored and mapped diverse, extensive, evolving realms of awareness, which are now becoming available to more people, deepening them into Spirit and ameliorating the destructive tendencies of materialism. More recently, social, psychological, and cognitive sciences have begun to clarify how civilization—with its languages, tools, stories, and constructed environments and institutions—shapes consciousness—*and* how individual and collective states of consciousness—and the interactions and conversations among conscious beings—influence and create culture and social systems. The more we explore these two, the more we discover that social systems and consciousness co-create each other and co-evolve. We will find increasingly potent evolutionary opportunities in the dynamics where these two powerful realities shape each other. As we engage those opportunities, we will become conscious agents of evolution, midwifing increasingly conscious and self-evolving people and social systems—which will constitute new forms of consciousness itself evolving.

7. IT'S ABOUT PROCESS. Evolution *is* process—or perhaps we should say a vast family of processes that together add up to creative development, unfolding complexity, and ever-emergent wholeness. How can we be conscious agents of such processes? How can we catalyze them, live into them, embody them? These are guiding questions for those of us wishing to become conscious manifestations of intentional evolution-in-action. Most leading-edge processes used in groups, organizations and communities involve many of the other dynamics listed here. They blend intentionality with a responsive "letting go of particular outcomes". They embody a trust in the capacity of living systems—under the right conditions—to call forth inspired, workable next steps. Creating those conditions is the task of the process worker, who holds a space for life's diversity to show up, interact, and learn in ways that welcome and empower breakthroughs. Reflecting on the creativity of the universe, we can imagine evolution pursuing and pushing the limits of an unspoken question: "What is actually possible here?" Evolutionary process workers use variations of that question to call forth the transformational energies of the people and systems they are working with. In the resulting conversations and interactive spaces, people explore their individual and collective dreams, passions, and circumstances and discover totally new possibilities they can work on or *be* together. As those possibilities get tested in the real world, evolution continues, with our conscious engagement, creating ever more space and energy for still newer possibilities...

8. LOVE AT THE CORE. The fact of evolution means we are all related. And the fact of gravity was the earliest way we were all called towards one another. Not just we humans, but all entities in the universe—all are expressions of one universe related, connected and attracted to one another. We have been kin since the infinitely intense birth of this universe, when we were obviously One but not separate enough to notice the fact. We all arose from the Source of that—whatever that may have been—and we are all made of stardust, literally. Two hundred million generations ago, our ancestors swam in the sea; today the chemistry of the sea flows through our veins. Our bodies contain great civilizations of highly specialized and synchronized single-celled beings, cousins of the trillions of microbes that populate the world around us. All humanity is one family, rich with diversity yet sharing one root. And the fundamental attraction that began 13.7 billion years ago when we were first torn apart has evolved into a richly varied dance of togetherness. Deep inside we know this, we resonate with one another, we are drawn into relationship, support, and celebration. Love is not something that needs to be added or built, only freed and nurtured, for it is our natural state.

We are All.

In This.

Together.

9. GRACE MOVES IT ALL. While our kinship is an ultimate truth, evolution is not static: It is urged on by Grace, the impulse to move from one state of wholeness into the next state of wholeness. At every moment, the universe is whole: there is a way in which, from the biggest perspective, everything fits. Yet included in that wholeness are things that at one level or another don't fit, creating a dynamic tension that seeks resolution—thereby calling forth the exact right wholeness (how perfect!). The resolution will be either healing into a former wholeness or transforming into a new wholeness, a new fit. This inborn tendency of reality and life to continually move towards wholeness is evolutionary Grace. A big part of evolutionary activism is consciously participating in that Grace—joining in, inviting, and facilitating that movement into whatever the next right wholeness may be. So Grace is the impetus through which the Creative Power of the Universe can and will forever find new forms and ways to be and do. Every urge we have to connect or to make things better is an expression of this unfolding reality, a reality-transforming Power that is as old as time.

Calling of Creation

First there was pure energy,
*   and from that...*
Evolution created matter
*   through which it shapes the conditions*
*   under which energy evolves—*
*   motion becoming heat, gravity*
*   mutating into electricity.*
Then evolution created life
*   through which it shapes the conditions*
*   under which matter evolves—*
*   DNA designing proteins, ecosystems*
*   altering atmospheres and oceans.*
Then evolution created conscious beings
*   through which it shapes the conditions*
*   under which life evolves—*
*   beliefs and solutions, visions and dreams*
*   cultures and technologies,*
*   transforming the world.*
We are That.
*   Through us, evolution is creating*
*   the capacity to consciously shape*
*   what is next.*
*   Through us, evolution itself*
*   is blossoming into consciousness.*

And to this we are called.

| ✳ |

Chapter Eight

Becoming evolution's
conscious weavers

Humanity—and Life itself perhaps—are at an evolutionary crossroads. What we do in the next few decades may determine whether or not any of our descendants are around for the next century, or forever. If we can better understand how evolution works, perhaps we can become more conscious agents of our own positive transformation, and thereby weavers of our world's next evolutionary step. In fact, these times call us to *become* evolution—or, rather, to become that aspect of evolution that is conscious of itself—for evolution is the Master Weaver, and we only do our weaving as part of that.

This essay introduces one of the most thought-provoking, mind-expanding practices of this Master Weaver—the interweaving of cooperation and competition into ever-more remarkable forms.

Living parts into living wholes

First, it helps to realize that evolution, as a whole, has tended to produce increasingly complex forms of life that include previous life-forms within them. What we once thought of as mere "building blocks" of today's organisms, for example, we now know had lives of their own, deep in the past.

The cells in our bodies—and in other multicellular organisms like sharks and maples—contain parts (mitochondria) that are now believed to have *Our bodies* started out as separate single-celled organisms that joined with other inde-*are ancient* pendent microbes to become the first *civilizations* nucleus-owning ancestors of our present *of microbes* cells. Other microbes came together eons ago as cooperative colonies, large and small. Some of these cooperative arrangements evolved into systems that were so successful that the original cellular colonists ended up totally dependent on one another. They could no longer survive on their own—just like us modern-day humans!

What started out as groups of cells became diverse tribes of cells which then evolved into virtual civilizations of cells—which we see all around us and think of as "plants and animals." For as evolution progressed, cells and groups of cells became more specialized in their tasks. In the process, they became simultaneously more diverse and more interconnected—forming, for example, hearts and kidneys—bodily organs that are analogous to the fuel distribution and waste processing systems we call society's "infrastructure." Probably the most complex organic systems on the planet are our nervous systems—not only our brains, but our whole web of nerves, including those nerve concentrations—those quasi-brains—that exist in our hearts and guts. The closer we look, the more we learn, the more miraculous it seems.

Cultural evolution

As suggested above, this increasing complexity of life didn't stop with biological evolution, but leapt into an entirely new realm of evolution: culture. With the advent of tool use, language, agriculture and writing, we humans created cultures and civilizations which, in their turn, have continually evolved. Family units combined into clans which combined into villages, which became tribes and then cities and then kingdoms, nations, empires, and now international institutions and networks, and meta-networks of networks like the Internet. Our cultures and knowledge continue to evolve—including and going beyond whatever came before, as Einstein's relativistic physics embraced and transcended Newton's mechanical physics.

The games of life: winning and shared destiny

In his book *Non-zero: The Logic of Human Destiny*, Robert Wright adds a fascinating twist to all this. He looks at evolution through the lens of game theory which, it turns out, has something useful to say about an amazing variety of fields.

Game theorists call a win-lose game (a game with a winner and loser) a "zero-sum" game: One winner plus one loser equals zero. On the other hand, they combine both win-win games (everybody wins) and lose-lose games (everybody loses) into a category called "non-zero-sum" games. For example, one winner plus one winner equals two winners (who are thus greater than zero). Likewise the two losers in a lose-lose game add up to "minus two", which is less than zero. So both win-win and lose-lose games are called non-zero-sum games by game theorists. This has interesting implications in evolution.

Non-zero-sum games usually look like collaboration, cooperation, mutuality, working together for the common good, etc., as well as shared suffering and shared destiny of all kinds. Zero-sum games look like competition, exploitation, destruction, etc., in which one organism or species benefits at the expense of others. Wright points out that these are not mutually exclusive dynamics, at least in the world of evolution. On closer examination, they are often complementary.

For example, although a predator-prey relationship seems like a win-lose game (the predator wins and the prey loses), there's actually more going on there. The fact that predators tend to take the weakest and sickest prey ends up strengthening a preyed-on herd or species, thus refashioning the predator-prey relationship into a win-win (non-zero-sum) game at the level of the herd or species. Likewise, if the predator didn't exist, the prey species would overpopulate, consume its environment, and die off (a well-known dynamic that should set off some alarm bells in our collective mind). And, of course, the predator species needs the prey species to continue in order for the predator species to have something to eat, so dynamics that sustain the prey species sustain the predator species, as well—and vice versa. Thus we find that the predator-prey relationship is, at the collective level, more win-win than it first seemed when viewed only at the individual level.

Evolution seeks synergy between competition and cooperation

Furthermore, an evolutionary development is often triggered by some threat or challenge—the prospect of losing one's life or position in life. The speed of the fox and the speed of the hare have evolved together, as the faster individuals in each species were more able to survive. This sort of "We become stronger through struggle" dynamic is often used to defend "free market capitalism"—which may be a valid comparison unless the strongest are left free to destroy everyone else in the market. But here in the dog-eat-dog marketplace we find another interesting marriage of zero and non-zero-sum games: Competition *between* corporations (and communities, too) has been one of the main drivers of increased cooperation *within* corporations (and communities). This cooperative impulse has been spreading outward such that "business ecosystems" are now springing up, involving clusters of companies in a given market—producers, suppliers, consumers, investors, etc.—all cooperating for collective benefit. "The more we work together as a team, the better we'll be able to beat the other teams."

Technology and cooperation

In another twist, Wright explores how new technologies can stimulate the emergence of non-zero-sum (win-win) arrangements. He describes how Shoshone Indians in what is now Nevada gathered their food. "For months at a time Shoshone families would go it alone, roaming the desert with a bag and a digging stick, searching for roots and seeds." But when they encountered a lot of rabbits, out would come "a tool too large for one family to handle—a net hundreds of feet long into which rabbits were herded before being clubbed to death. On such occasions ... a dozen normally autonomous families would come together briefly" to collaborate in the rabbit "harvest," followed by a feast and celebration.

In a more ominous example, nuclear weapons in the hands of superpowers ultimately created the non-zero-sum game called Mutually Assured Destruction (MAD)—the terrifying lose-lose prospect of global thermonuclear holocaust used for "deterrence"—which engendered a surprising amount of cooperation between the superpowers after the close call of the Cuban Missile Crisis of 1962, even as they competed and dominated in their spheres of influence.

Probably the most familiar current example of technology's birthing of win-win games is the way the Web, cell phones, and other telecommunications are creating whole new economies—including new forms of intellectual property—that are fundamentally based on cooperation rather than competition. Those who survive best in these new economies are those who cooperate best, and help others cooperate (such as Google and EBay).

What evolution is doing

Wright's key insight is that evolution has, for billions of years, been steadily weaving *increasingly inclusive non-zero-sum games*—especially cooperative arrangements among life forms, both biological and cultural. From the earliest little cellular patches and colonies, on up through the fabric of multicellular organism evolution into the increasingly complex and inclusive global garment of cooperation and competition woven into today's densely interconnected world, the evolutionary loom hums along.

But the evolutionary game is changing, because we don't have any higher-level ecosystem for competitive dynamics to play out in. The final level of inclusivity is everyone, the whole world. Everyone wins or everyone loses. The "other" is vanishing. We are all in this together. We all live downstream.

In other words, we now find ourselves faced with the ultimate lose-lose possibility—the destruction of our biosphere, without which all human games—if not all life—will cease. Now that we are operating at this global level, more and more of our favorite win-lose games are turning into lose-lose games. In other words, previously useful zero-sum games are becoming deadly non-zero-sum games. War is becoming obsolete. Mindless exploitation is becoming self-defeating.

Non-zero-sum means we all win together or we all lose together. Welcome to globalization.

Manipulative, biased news media are blinding and endangering us all. Faced with the option of all of us losing together or all of us winning together, we now enter our "final exam" in human evolution—and possibly biological evolution—on Earth. We get to pass, or fail, together.

Luckily, technologies of cooperation—ways of facilitating win-win dynamics—are rapidly developing. Furthermore, at the leading edge of these developments are technologies that embrace competition for its gifts even while enfolding competition within the larger need for cooperation—because we need competition in order to remain healthy and continue evolving.

The more competition is engaged in by willing partners who seek mutual benefit through that process—as happens in the highest level of sport where "opponents" use their contest to bring out their "personal best"—the more synergy will exist between competition and cooperation. Likewise, the more competition serves to keep cooperation from getting lazy (as in conformity, groupthink, and old habits that resist needed change), the more synergy we will have between competition and cooperation. And the more the cooperative spirit prevents competition from becoming "cut-throat"—and exploitation (as in the use of nature and people) from degrading Life—the more synergy we will have between competition and cooperation.

Our task

In evolution, both competition and cooperation ultimately serve the wellbeing of the whole. We are called to do both consciously and wisely, thereby becoming the evolutionary vehicle that will carry us through the next century.

Our challenge is to get very good at this dance. From the perspective of billions of years of evolution—arriving at this critical time of major breakdown or breakthrough—that's the name of the game right now. Our task is to figure out how to weave every viewpoint, every interest, every species into a fully inclusive win-win game that we can all play long-term, spiced with—but not ruled by—ongoing competition.

"We are all in this together." That statement has always represented our highest challenge. It has been spoken in various forms by most great religions. And recently it has been hailed as fact by systems thinkers, ecologists and quantum physicists. But "We are all in this together" is now more than an exhortation or a static fact. It is a dynamic evolutionary reality that we will all be living out, one way or another, as we pass this evolutionary crossroads. One road leads to the ultimate dead-end. The other leads through conscious, continuous transformation of ourselves and our societies into ever wiser manifestations of this truth. We are all in this together.

As more of us join in finding ways to be true to the fact of our shared destiny, we collectively *become* the growing edge of evolution as it weaves its way into ever richer win-win games, hopefully for millennia to come.

First of All

First of all, there is nothing
here in our World but
Stardust, Sunshine, and Original Radiance.

The Story is simple
and lies at the Heart
of all beginnings:

Original Radiance birthed primordial energy
which birthed primordial substance like dew
all over the first eons of Kosmos.

Substance, converging, birthed stars
which, burning and bursting, birthed
a blossoming fellowship of complexity
a reign of stardust madly dancing.

The dancing fellowship of stardust twingled
into increasingly complex forms,
whose combinations and conversations
soon became the World we see
and are.

And every twist and turn, dash,
delight and upwelling of such real, riotous
life—our world—is fueled by Sunlight.

And it is all, all, all
the endlessly expressive face
of Original Radiance
evolving, embracing
all matter, energy, space, time and pattern,
transcribed into landscapes and events
by its endlessly evocative partner,
Consciousness,
master of manifestation,
consummate storyteller.

Yes.
And we are That.
And That is All There Is:

The Holy Trinity of
Stardust, Sunshine, and Original Radiance
dancing forever now
in the spreading Stories of Consciousness.

| ✳ |

Reflections on

Strategy and Tactics

Chapter Nine

Learning from our evolutionary past into our evolutionary future

A hundred years ago George Santayana suggested, "Those who cannot remember the past are condemned to repeat it." Most people interpret this to mean that we should remember history. But Santayana didn't say history. He said "the past." That applies to everything from yesterday's *faux pas* to the 13.7 billion year sweep of evolution.[4]

I see evolution as the story and process of all developments in the universe up until now. For us humans, evolution embraces the cosmic story, the story of our solar system and our Earth, the story of Life, and the story of Humankind and our many civilizations.

So what evolutionary events might Santayana want us to learn from, were he alive today and knew our deep-time past?

---

[4] We now call this Big History, as described in Chapter One.

Perhaps the most important past experience we don't want to repeat is that suffered by the vast majority of species that have ever walked, swum, flown or crawled upon this earth—*extinction*. It would also be wise to avoid that most typical fate of great civilizations—*collapse*.

So what do we need to do to avoid these? From one evolutionary perspective, the answer is *wake up!*

The universe, life, and human history have been unfolding in a rough-and-tumble, more or less unconscious fashion for quite a while. Today we have a chance to change that. If we can learn what evolution has been doing and do our part of it more consciously—with more wisdom, compassion, and choice—*in time*—we may be able to avoid fatal disasters like collapse and extinction.

After all, one of the main reasons evolution developed awareness in the first place was to enable organisms like us (and bacteria, fish, and foxes) to anticipate dangers and opportunities and thus to take timely and useful action.

To the extent we, as a species, learn to consciously and wisely do what evolution has done largely by trial and error, we will be practicing *conscious evolution*, itself a radically new evolutionary phenomenon. We will *be* evolution, come awake.

This is not to say that we can or should be the entirety of evolution being fully conscious of everything it does. Such total awareness is not necessary, desirable, or possible. So what *does* conscious evolution mean?

As individuals, we consider ourselves conscious even though the vast majority of our physical, mental and emotional processes function outside our awareness. We think of ourselves as conscious because so much of what we think, feel and do *does* involve at least *some* level or form of consciousness. Furthermore, through various efforts and engagements, we can become *more* conscious in various areas of our lives.

This is particularly important when some aspect of our life is in need of change. We get signals—discomforts, pains, distresses, things not going right—even hopes, dreams, and longings. Such disturbances are signs that our unconscious, automatic ways—our instincts, habits, assumptions, and business as usual behaviors—are no longer serving our full wellbeing. Something different needs to happen. At such times, it behooves us to pay attention—through reflection, problem solving, therapy, meditation, etc.— to bring up through the subconscious into conscious awareness whatever is *We can help consciousness respond to disturbance* not working or whatever new possibilities are trying to surface, where they can be intentionally, intelligently addressed. Once we have addressed them, once the shift into new ways has happened, our consciousness can relax or explore something else.

This on-and-off dynamic of consciousness plays a vital role on behalf of life—not to colonize all of life, but to respond to signs that something about our lives needs to shift into a more life-serving, healthy pattern. Once we make the shift, the new pattern can become automatic, freeing our attention to move on to other things until the next time the pattern needs adjustment.

So when I say that we are evolution becoming conscious of itself, I mean that we are a *part of the evolutionary process* (a) that has awakened to what it is doing, (b) that applies conscious choice to aspects of itself that could be more healthy, life-serving, or meaningful and (c) that learns from its experience, consciously evolving what it believes and does to make more sense, over and over.

So what can we say about what evolution has been doing that might be useful to those of us who are trying to make a difference, here and now?

Well, the most general understanding is that evolution happens through the *interactions* of diverse *entities* in particular *contexts* that are more or less nurturing and more or less challenging. These interactions generate the two great phenomena of evolution—continuity and novelty—the dynamics through which things persist and the dynamics through which new things show up. One of the novelties that has emerged from the evolutionary process is our human *consciousness*, which is now a major factor in what happens next.

Evolution responds to big challenges with creative leaps—which usually wipe out something that seemed pretty solid before—and then provides ways to sustain its novel creations until they get challenged by some new circumstance. Consciousness, too, goes through this same process. It is called "learning."

Our efforts to be conscious about all this will involve initiatives and questions like these, all of which overlap one another in useful ways:

1. Becoming more conscious of *entities*—more aware of the diverse entities we are dealing with—ourselves, first of all, and then other people, animals, plants, places, organizations, cultures, countries, human systems, and natural systems. What do we know—or need to know—about who they are, what their story is, what they need, what their unique gifts are? How can we be wiser about who we welcome and who we exclude, and how? What can we learn about diversity and its power to make a difference? How can we deepen our understanding of the larger living systems and entities we are part of, and our role in them and in their own evolution?

Evolution happens through the INTERACTIONS of diverse ENTITIES in particular CONTEXTS

2. Becoming more conscious of *interactions*—more consciously creative about the interactions we engage in and co-create with and for others. How are we communicating? What's the best way to deal with conflict here? Are our economies set up so that people and nature are well served—individually, locally, and globally—by the production, exchange, and disposal of goods and the provision of services? Do the rules of the game help self-interested individuals, groups, companies, and countries interact in ways that support the wellbeing of the whole world? Are our cities, conferences, and networks organized so participants can usefully and creatively interact? Is what we are doing—

especially our activism—serving the emergence of greater understanding, relationship, and positive possibility? What power dynamics are at work? How can we interact creatively *with* whatever we find?

3. Becoming more conscious of *contexts*—more alert to the powerful settings we are (and could be) living and working in. What is the culture and history here? What dreams and inquiries do people have, or might they have, with the right engagement from us? What powerful intention could guide us in this particular moment or event? What is the impact of the spaces we occupy, such as the presence or absence of walls and nature, rows and circles, food and smiles, guns and flags? What can we do to better understand and support the human and natural systems that support us? Can we all get the information we need and fairly participate? How might we most creatively handle dissonance, disturbance, and crisis? What can we learn about creating a fruitful balance between nurturance and challenge?

4. Becoming more conscious of *consciousness*—more aware of the role of consciousness in shaping what's happening. To what extent are we fully present to the Now—and to the past (stories, patterns, forms, memories) and future (expectations, trajectories, possibilities, longings) contained within it? What else do we need to be aware of in this situation? What unexamined assumptions and values underlie what we and others are doing and saying? What stories are we telling ourselves, or others—or are we being told? What other stories might serve Life better? Are our social systems set up to support our collective awareness, intelligence, wisdom, and choice? Are we humble in the face of uncertainty and wonder-full in the face of Mystery?

Another overlapping evolutionary dynamic lies at the heart of what many scientists call "evolutionary directionality". It provides perhaps the most fundamental guidance for our era, informing all of the above inquiries. It has two dimensions:

A. Evolving complexity. Evolution proceeds largely by simple entities, interactions, contexts, and modes of consciousness combining and differentiating in novel ways to become more complex, nuanced and capable together than they were separately.

Functional complexity evolves as self-interest becomes aligned with the wellbeing of the whole

B. Evolving self-interest. In life, this coming-together-into-new-wholes—this increasing complexity—succeeds when the self-interested behavior of the previously independent entities ends up furthering the wellbeing of the new whole they comprise. As single cells found more ways to work together for mutual benefit, multicellular organisms appeared. As humans found more ways to work together for mutual benefit, societies formed.

As human civilizations have rapidly complexified, new entities, interactions, contexts and modes of consciousness have emerged. For better and worse, we now live in a world profoundly shaped by our own co-created complexities, a human-made world embedded in, but attempting to dominate and restrain, the evolved complexities of the natural world.

As we have expanded, our needs and impacts have become globally interwoven with all of humanity and the whole biosphere. Human and non-human elements are becoming one vast integrated whole. As our self-interested human technologies, populations, systems, and activities increasingly impact the non-human parts of Earth—air, water, land, and life—the wellbeing of the whole is increasingly challenged.

Santayana might step in here to remind us of the past: Evolution tells us clearly that such a perilous situation will not continue. Collapse and extinction loom.

Many parts of the Whole Earth—species, ecosystems, cultures (especially primary or indigenous peoples)—are being driven to extinction. The more we—especially the privileged among us—ignore our impacts and use technology to ensure our welfare and development at the expense of the Earth and Others, the more out-of-equilibrium our situation will become, and the more violently nature and Others will ultimately respond to bring the overall system into a new balance.

Extreme climate change, resource depletion, new and expanding diseases, social disturbances—even our own self-destructive innovations—all are evolutionary challenges arising from our failure to align and pursue our self-interest in the context of the wellbeing of the Whole.

As a whole, humanity is now challenged to use our emerging evolutionary consciousness to co-create new systems, interactions, contexts, and modes of consciousness to meet the challenges we have created for ourselves, in ways that nurture the wellbeing of the whole we are part of.

Here are initiatives that serve systemic awareness, systemic health, and systemic learning

Evolutionary initiatives

The previous paragraph identifies one of the most important guiding principle with which to evaluate activist efforts. Our most effective evolutionary creations will be initiatives that serve this capacity to nurture the wellbeing of the whole through the activities of self-interested entities. A major evolutionary action project involves cataloging, mapping, and strategizing the wide range of such evolutionary innovations, to clarify directions for evolutionary activism. For now, here are some initial approaches and examples, organized into initiatives that serve systemic awareness, systemic health, and systemic learning:

Systemic awareness. Resources and activities that make us increasingly aware of the social, technological, and natural systems we are part of, so that we can experience first-hand those systems operating through us, and alter our beliefs and behaviors as part of evolving those systems into more benign forms. In my own case, I have been influenced in this way by these remarkable resources, among others:

- The art of Chris Jordan visualizes the impact of our consumerism - *chrisjordan.com*

- Joanna Macy's work embeds us in living systems from the inside out - *joannamacy.net*

- Annie Leonard's "The Story of Stuff" video vividly depicts the cycle of production and consumption - *storyofstuff.com*

- Paul Ehrlich and Robert Ornstein's *New World New Mind* describes our creation of impacts which we have not evolved to comprehend and respond to - both print and free downloadable versions are available from *ishkbooks.com/NWNM/TOC.html*

- Lois Mark Stalvey's *The Education of a WASP* describes chapter by chapter one woman's realization of racism in and around her - *books.google.com/books ?id=ENBf15XV6soC&sitesec=reviews&source=gbs_na vlinks_s*

- Michael Dowd's *Thank God for Evolution* embeds us in a sacred deep time Great Story of the universe, alive in every moment - *thankgodforevolution.com*

- David Gershon's *Low Carbon Diet* provides a way to radically reduce our carbon footprint through awareness and mutual support - *empowermentinstitute.net/lcd*

- The many essays of Donella Meadows have an uncanny ability to translate systems into everyday realities and language - *sustainer.org/dhm_archive*
- The simplicity movement makes it enjoyable to be conscious and responsible about our choices as consumers - *simpleliving.net*
- The new Constitution of Ecuador recognizes the rights of nature - *celdf.org/Default.aspx?tabid=548*

Systemic health. New systems, technologies, principles, and movements that create contexts within which our self-interested everyday actions as individuals, groups, and organizations naturally add up to a healthy world of healthy individuals and healthy communities. Approaches I have found that may be useful for this—especially for evolving economics—include:

- "Full-cost accounting" and "internalized costs" that incorporate social and environmental impacts in the prices of goods and services, thus enabling the free market to function benignly instead of destructively - *en.wikipedia.org/wiki/Full_cost_accounting*
- Redefining Progress offers new community and national economic indicators that measure real environmental and social wellbeing, to replace or complement monetary measures like GDP - *rprogress.org*
- The movement reclaiming democracy from corporations, e.g., to limit their influence on elections, reverse their legal "personhood," reinstitute revocable corporate charters delineating their public

benefit, etc., so that their impact is more contribu-
tory than parasitic -

ratical.org/corporations/ReadingLinks.html#Links

- Green America offers an exemplary base for socially
  responsible investment, stockholder activism, and
  corporate responsibility - *greenamericatoday.org*
- Total Corporate Responsibility goes beyond the
  "triple bottom line" (social and ecological as well as
  financial success) to take political action for greater
  social and ecological responsibility by all comparable corporations -

iccr.org/news/press_releases/dixonspeachb092304.PDF

- For-benefit "B corporations" and low-profit limited
  liability corporations (L3Cs) move beyond for-
  profit and non-profit corporate forms to permit the
  making of profit within the context of explicitly
  serving the public good - *bcorporation.net* and
  gaebler.com/L3C-Business-Structures.htm
- Natural Capitalism incorporates many of the above
  innovations as well as technological innovations to
  make capitalism an ecologically benign expression
  of nature - *natcap.org*
- Business Alliance for Local Living Economies
  (BALLE) helps empower local communities to become more successful and self-reliant, thereby re-
  ducing transport-related energy use, building community, and shortening the feedback loops that make
  a healthy system more resilient to environmental and
  economic shocks - *livingeconomies.org*

- The Precautionary Principle suggests that any technology demonstrate its safety and benign ecological impact before it is applied out in the environment - *en.wikipedia.org/wiki/Precautionary_principle*

- A Pattern Language for Sustainability describes some interrelated design principles which together paint a whole picture of a sustainable economy, providing guidance for organizing and curricula -

  conservationeconomy.net

- "Open" participatory approaches to all kinds of creative and collaborative work—including

  open source
  en.wikipedia.org/wiki/Open_source
  open content
  en.wikipedia.org/wiki/Open_content
  open design
  en.wikipedia.org/wiki/Open_design etc.

- Permaculture provides design guidance for productive ecosystems (gardens, buildings, communities) appropriate to a given place -
  en.wikipedia.org/wiki/Permaculture

Systemic learning. Approaches that support the ability of public collectives—communities, movements, and societies—to learn, to grow in wisdom and vision, to act coherently, and to change themselves in response to new insights and conditions. Some of the approaches that most appeal to me include:

- Empowered citizen deliberative councils and wisdom councils in which randomly selected citizens explore the state of their community or the demands of a particular issue and develop thoughtful guidance for leaders and their fellow citizens - *co-intelligence.org/CDCUsesAndPotency.html*
- Advanced forms of whole-system inquiry and dialogue that generate collective intelligence and community wisdom, as described at *bit.ly/Particip Methods* and in Peggy Holman, *et al, The Change Handbook* - *thechangehandbook.com*
- Networked participatory movement databases like WISER Earth which help activists find useful information, relevant organizations, and one another, and to collaborate in areas of shared interest - *wiserearth.org*
- Processes like the Earth Charter movement which engage thousands of people to articulate a more collaborative relationship among people and with nature - *earthcharterinaction.org/about_charter.html*
- Journalism that Matters which models how a profession in crisis can redefine itself and co-evolve new forms that fit better with current realities - *journalismthatmatters.org/newsecology*
- Storyfield activism directly addresses the larger narrative fields—generated by movies, novels, journalism, education, video games, advertising, politics, and more—that shape what whole populations think is real, good, and possible - *storyfieldconference.net*

There is much more to conscious evolution than these. But this list can introduce you to how the evolutionary perspective can influence how we think about the work we do on behalf of the world and the future generations of all species. *It can guide us towards activism that transforms current social systems, cultures, and technologies into a coherent, healthy, self-evolving civilization that can see humanity and its larger community of Life through the next several centuries on Earth.*

That Great Evolving Power

That great Power that explodes the stars above,
that same Power breaks open hearts to love;
that evolving Power is what God is thinking of;
as His Power of Emergence
  welcomes newness to the world.

That great Power that founded gravity;
that same Power that woke the world to see;
that evolving Power that has woven you and me:
that Power of Emergence
  is now weaving through our world.

That great Power that made atoms out of quarks,
that same Power calls the music out of larks;
that evolving Power gave us meaning out of marks:
we can hear the Power of Emergence
  rising round us in our world.

That great Power, it helps the seeker find,
that same Power ignites the human mind;
that great evolving Power shapes
  whatever minds design;
yes, the Power of Emergence
  working through us in this world.

That great Power that gardens us with pain;
that same Power that seeds the hurricane;
this great evolving Power
　　summons green life out of rain—
yes, the Power of Emergence
　　brings life whirling through our world.

That great Power that is stardust everywhere;
that same Power stirred our stardust into care;
that evolving Power's making stardust more aware—
yes, the Power of Emergence
　　is now waking up our world.

That great Power that birthed the universe;
that same Power drives our times from bad to worse;
that evolving Power makes us
　　strain and sweat and curse
as the Power of Emergence
　　births more blessings to our world.

That great Power made great order yesterday;
that same Power uses chaos as its clay;
that evolving Power always finds its mystery way
and that Power of Emergence is within us,
here among us,　　here around us,
here to grow us,　　here to guide us
in our lives　　and in our world.

| ✳ |

Chapter Ten

A "Big Story" evolutionary fitness program

As a civilization we face challenges to our usual ways of doing things—to our social, economic, and political systems—in fact, to all our systems, and even to our cultural stories and technologies. Fifty, 100, 250 years from now, there is no way that civilization will look anything like it does today. We are going to be radically different, one way or another.

Some of those possibilities are thrilling, such as creating a truly sustainable, just, wise, enjoyable civilization for the first time on Earth. Other possibilities are downright terrifying. For example, by continuing on our current path we could push climate change so far, we could make the climate so hot, cold, and/or wildly variable that Earth becomes unlivable for most complex life forms, including ourselves. Still other possibilities are thrilling or terrifying depending on who you are. For example, "transhumanists" and others look forward to the exponential growth of technology ("the singularity") and its integration with or transcendence of our biological bodies and minds, to create a new and more potent, resilient, long-lived species—a prospect that seems horribly alienating and even arrogant to people grounded in the organic nature of humanity.

Whatever else we believe, or know, or do or don't do to address the crises of our times, there are three overarching fundamental realities that will shape what happens for all humans in the next 50-250 years—and *all* of them have to do with evolution. Here are the fundamental realities of our times, which are fundamental realities of life:

1. Those living beings, communities, and species that do not *fit* do not survive.
2. Those that *change to fit the realities of their situation—or alter their situation in ways that fit larger contextual realities—* do survive.
3. *Conscious* living entities thrive and sustain themselves into the deep future to the exact extent that they continue to *craft their fit* with elegance and wisdom.

In short, the only way we'll make it is to get real about evolution—about our role in the evolutionary process and the role of evolution in our world, our lives, our destiny.

The only way we'll make it is to wake up into the evolutionary perspective and start acting in ways that make evolutionary sense.

Our ignoring evolution does not make us any less subject to evolution's laws and creative potentials than the still-evolving finches seen by Darwin in the Galápagos Islands 173 years ago, or the long-gone dinosaurs our children love to worship, or the rapidly changing viruses and bacteria medical science works so hard to stay ahead of.

The quality of our conscious choice to fit will determine our survival and evolution

We're all subject to evolution. We humans are part of this evolving world, and we will survive and flourish to the extent we find new ways to fit well with this world and partner well with the emergent possibilities that are always gestating within it.

The consciousness with which we find our fit—the wisdom and choicefulness with which we make our way into the future—will determine our survival and who we become as our journey unfolds.

This consciousness, this wisdom, this choicefulness are no accident. They, too, emerged out of the creative dynamic interactivity of our world—that miraculous process we now call *evolution*. Our ability to observe, to think, to know, and to envision and choose—the very capacities we call consciousness and intelligence—these are emergent properties of evolution. They came out of the intensely interactive past, the 13.7 billion year great star story and life story of evolution.

Most important of all, they are in the process of evolving right now, in this moment as you read this, in this community, in this country, on this planet, today. And they will continue to evolve *through us all* after you stop reading this, as you go about your daily life, as we all go about our daily lives. As long as we exist, we will evolve.

Everything we notice, think, feel, do, create—our consciousness, our knowledge, our cultures and social systems, our technologies, our stories—all the unique realities of our individual and collective humanness are now evolving at an unprecedented rate. *And well they should, because their evolution is the key to our survival. How we shape these realities, how they shape us, and how we use them to shape our world will determine if and how we flourish or vanish as communities and as a civilization.*

Our 21st century predicament did not just happen to us. We have created the conditions in our world that now challenge us so thoroughly. We have done and are doing things out of our perceived self-interest that are degrading or destroying the life-support systems upon which we depend. We will only make it to the extent we wake up to this great evolutionary karmic fact: We reap what we sow.

Our capacities have evolved from shaping hand tools, vehicles, communities and landscapes to shaping nanotubes, spaceships, global economies and climates. We have evolved to shape the evolution of our world, where we are now, arguably, the dominant evolutionary force.

So the question now isn't *whether* we will evolve—because we will and are evolving, no matter what. The question is rather *how consciously and wisely we will go about evolving*. Because all our individual and collective evolution will only *serve us* to the extent it helps us *fit*—to engage with our world and one another in harmonious, mutual, co-creative ways.

If we fail to *harmonize our individual and corporate self-interest with the wellbeing of the whole of life,* we will soon be gone. We have become too powerful for it to be otherwise. This is not a fate to which we are doomed. It is a challenging opportunity to which the evolutionary process has brought us. And rising to that challenge will constitute a heroic evolutionary leap—*one we can only take consciously.* The more consciously we leap, the more likely we'll succeed with the least unnecessary suffering and the most powerful learning and thrill.

That is why an evolutionary worldview is absolutely essential for humanity in this century. *We are not separate from evolution.* All the changes we make and live through are evolution happening now, right here, through us. To the extent we make those changes consciously—aware of the big picture of who we are, of the Great Story we are part of and what we are doing in it—we not only vastly increase our chances for success, but we become a piece of evolution itself waking up into consciousness of itself, and taking responsibility for itself. *That* is a brand new thing under the sun.

There is something important going on in this, something that seems to have escaped the notice of most of humanity, but which has been going on for almost 14 billion years. We humans—and all our non-human brothers and sisters—are living manifestations of a Story that has been around, in one form or another, a long, long time. And now we get one chance to wake up and become the Story suddenly conscious of itself. Our challenge is to wake up fully enough, and in time, to become what evolution is obviously trying to make us: A conscious, wise version of vibrant Evolution.

It would be a tragedy to waste this opportunity by clinging to business as usual just because it is familiar. That would mean evolution would have to try waking up through robots—or perhaps through raccoons with intelligence, opposable thumbs, and a lot of complex garbage left behind by a nearly wise species that almost made it. It is much more thrilling to awaken and tackle the job of conscious evolution with everything we've got, and pull off one of the greatest miracles in the history of the universe.

We need to attend to three key dynamics to practice conscious evolution

To pull it off we need to focus on three interrelated evolutionary dynamics which, if we apply them wisely at all levels of our existence—to our lives, to the cultures and systems we live in, and to our knowledge and technologies—we will generate the world we want and transform ourselves into who we most want to be. These three basic, profoundly useful evolutionary insights are:

1. Interacting diversity generates change.
2. Alignment with reality as it really is generates survival.
3. Harmonizing the self-interest of the parts with the wellbeing of the whole sustains vibrantly evolving complexity.

We can expand each of these deceptively simple principles into dozens of related guidelines, programs, and ways of living and organizing society. They constitute a three-part formula for promoting evolutionary fitness for humanity, from our personal lives to our global civilization.

Underlying them all is a deep spiritual reality: All the dramatic bustle of evolution is actually *wholeness transforming itself into new forms of wholeness*. I believe that as we apply these three very practical evolutionary dynamics to ourselves and our world, we will become increasingly aware of this metaphysical truth. We will come to notice that this is what is going on in every moment, every thought, every response. Then, as we gradually and thoroughly wake up to ourselves and our world as Wholeness transforming Itself, we will simply *become* evolution, seamlessly and joyously unfolding. We will have arrived home to the role for which we were made and thereby become whole.

A Larger Force Works Through Us

The universe that sees
itself through these
two eyes of mine
has learned to shine

through us its creativity
on each day's rich nativity —
worlds of glass and worlds of gold,
worlds beyond what we behold —

larger, smaller, faster, new,
our power takes a darker hue,
as wisdom hungers for a breeze
to bring our power to its knees

in prayer before the Life that sees
itself through these eyes and *the trees.*

| ✳ |

Chapter Eleven

The strategic synergy of individual and collective

In my circles I often hear people say that "it all starts with the individual", in the sense that we each have to do our own developmental and get-your-life-together work in order to secure enough awareness, health, and personal organization to truly contribute to the betterment of our community and world.

This individualistic assumption collides with my own activist sense that individuals are shaped by their social systems and circumstances, and that it is often important to start at the collective level—creating support communities, political and economic systems, new cultural stories, conversational processes, technologies, etc., that facilitate personal development, healthy behavior, and positive individual contributions.

Of course, both individual and collective approaches are needed—and not separately, but together, because they support and influence each other.

Whether we assume that "it all starts with the individual" or "individuals are shaped by their social systems and circumstances", we miss the point. In reality individuals influence collective awareness, functioning and evolution *and* collective systems influence individual consciousness, functioning and evolution.

Individual and collective capacities and dynamics constitute a feedback cycle which doesn't *start* anywhere. Or perhaps I should say that this feedback cycle starts everywhere. (This is similar to it being more useful to talk about leaderful groups rather than leaderless groups. Both are true, but the framing invites different consciousness and behavior.) This realization about the feedback and synergy between the individual and collective opens the consciousness of evolutionary activists to strategies that maximize the evolution of *both*.

Our challenge, then, might be stated as:

> How can we enhance
> and/or use
> individual capacities
> in ways that support healthy groups and societies
> *so that*
> those enhanced groups and societies
> can then better enhance
> and/or use

collective capacities
to enhance individual wellbeing and evolution
    so that
those enhanced individuals
can enhance their groups and societies and world,
    on and on and on
      in a continuing upward
        evolutionary spiral...?

Here are some responses to get us thinking...

- We can form **spiritual communities** (from *sanghas* to prayer groups to nature spirit circles) to enhance individual spiritual development.

- We can gather in **communities of practice or inquiry** that enhance our individual capacity to learn and do the kind of work we need to do.

- We can organize **support groups** that enhance individual behavioral change, such as decreasing our carbon footprint. David Gershon's *Low Carbon Diet* book and program offers a superlative example.

- We can do therapy, meditation, groupwork and other **personally transformative practices** that enable us to collaborate better in groups and take our own power co-creatively in collective initiatives to transform dysfunctional systems.

- We can practice **group support for individual behaviors that enhance collective intelligence.** Open Space, World Cafe, Appreciative Inquiry, and wikis all do that, powerfully inviting individuals to interact in generative ways. Participating individuals often shift in ways that enhance their awareness and behavior outside of the specific engagement. They begin thinking and behaving in more creative, collaborative ways— and sometimes they even go on to convene Open Spaces, World Cafes, Appreciative Inquiries and wikis in their own lives, communities, and work.

Only together can we realize our profound human potential and evolutionary fitness

- We can create and publicize **data displays, art works, and stories that show people their place in—and impact on—larger systems** they're part of. Such media are derived from our collective capacities to fathom and gather data about such systemic dynamics using computers, sensors, scientific research, crowdsourcing, etc. Thus they constitute a collective impact on individual consciousness. Often they inspire individual participation in collective information gathering (from scientific work to participating in crowdsourcing activities) that can, in turn, further uplift individual systemic and evolutionary awareness... which then results in *more* collectively healthy behaviors by individuals...

- We can promote or organize **citizen deliberative councils and other conversational civic practices** which include diverse voices. By creatively using diversity, these conversations end up manifesting a higher level of *group* awareness and development than the average (and even sometimes highest) developmental awareness of its members. Imagine a group becoming wiser than its members, instead of dumber! We can advocate democratic innovations that use such groups to create policies and social systems that raise up a whole community's or society's functioning so that it acts as if it is much, much more aware and intelligent than its individual citizens. The presence of such groups—often just randomly selected ordinary people who are helped to learn about a topic and to hear one another well—can help enlighten those members of the community or society that observe their activities or read their collective statements. Then *those* citizens become potential future members of subsequent citizen deliberative councils, enabling *those* councils to rise even higher, taking the community with them...

- We can advocate and institute **economic indicators and "full cost accounting" protocols** that internalize the full social and ecological costs of products and services into the prices of those products and services. With these innovations the "invisible hand" of the free market is motivated to produce socially and environmentally benign and healthy collective outcomes. (When the primary accounting is money and profit, the invisible hand does everything it can to get someone else—like the government, the poor, the environment, or future generations—to deal with the messes it makes while it makes its money.) Guided by realistic full-cost accounting prices, self-interested individuals and corporations start behaving in ways that serve the wellbeing of the whole (which of course includes them). Individual innovators and entrepreneurs would create products and services that enhance the capacity of the market to do its life-serving work.

Ultimately, we want a society where Peggy Holman's brilliant guideline, "Take responsibility for what you love as an act of service", *automatically* serves the whole. This has both individual and collective dimensions. The individual dimension is each person's awareness and attunement to "where my passion and gifts meet the world's needs." The collective dimension resides in the design of the cultures, technologies, communities, and systems (social/economic/political) that people live in, which constrain, guide, and inspire individual behaviors so that life-serving activities and outcomes happen quite naturally and inevitably. These two dynamics support each other, making a world that is truly inviting and vibrant to be part of.

Journey Power Story Questions

What is the Journey that shapes this moment?
What is the Journey that shapes today?
What is the Journey that shapes tomorrow?
What is the Journey that opens the Way?

We are the Journey that makes this moment.
We're on the Journey that shapes today.
We'll make the Journey that wakes tomorrow,
Living our Journey to open the Way.

What is the Power that shapes this moment?
What is the Power that calls forth today?
Show us the Power that shapes tomorrow.
Tender our Power to open the Way.

Knowing the Power that shapes each moment,
We have the Power to free each day.
Call forth the Power to gift tomorrow
And live in the Power that opens the Way.

What is the Story that shapes this moment?
What is the Story that frees today?
What kind of Story will gift the morrow?
What sort of Story will open the Way?

Listening to Stories that shape this moment.
We share our Stories to free today.
We weave the Stories that bring tomorrow,
Welcoming Stories to open the Way.

What is the Question to open this moment?
What potent Question will wake us today?
Give us new Questions to birth tomorrow,
Starting with Questions to open the Way.

Alive are the Stories that shape this moment.
Alive is the Power to shape today.
Called to a Journey that shakes tomorrow,
Life asks us Questions to open the Way.

| ✳ |

Chapter Twelve

The role of conversation in evolution

Evolution and conversation are close cousins. Both involve the unfolding of potentially transformative interactions among diverse entities.

If we want to consciously and intentionally change our social systems — if we want them to evolve in ways that make sense — then we need to talk together about it. The more inclusive, wise and productive our conversations are, the more powerful and positive the changes will be. It is no accident that the conversational dimension of our work is usually called "process". Conversation is our way of being in process and evolving together. Given the many crises that are emerging today, high quality conversation is an essential evolutionary force.

Evolution is about change. Anyone doing social change work, anyone trying to improve conditions, anyone trying to empower, succeed, innovate, heal, strengthen, renew, transform, enlighten—or even conquer or destroy—is engaged in evolutionary work. We are all evolutionary participants, every day.

Evolution is happening now

Ultimately change is happening all the time—and we're all involved—whether we notice it or not, whether we want to or not. Some very stable-seeming things—like mountains and stars—are changing in ways or at speeds we cannot easily see, or are made up of a dance of smaller changes. Furthermore, evolution doesn't stop: Changes over here in my world evoke changes over there in yours. We keep striving to get to a place that is more comfortable, more enjoyable, more successful, more whole—changing things for everyone else as we do. All the little changes in our personal lives add up to bigger changes in our shared world—just look at climate change for a vivid example. Those big changes then influence our personal lives and shape our neighbors, the economy, and the future of our planet.

We are on a cusp of unprecedented crises caused by the obliviousness with which we use our awesome collective power. With climate change, extreme economic imbalances, the degradation of democracy, dangerous technological developments and many other dangers and collective stupidities, we're rapidly co-creating a 'change or die' situation. These crises will bring changes we can barely imagine. We have brought ourselves to a brink of both calamity and transcendence at a global level. Business as usual—the source of our security—is now becoming ever more clearly The Problem. So we find ourselves blessed/cursed (both!) with a marriage of opportunity and necessity: We can and we must transform ourselves and our social systems into a truly wise force for conscious evolution—a whole new way of being a civilization.

That is why we are here. It is the next chapter of our evolutionary story.

The changes we need involve developing our collective intelligence, consciousness and wisdom to transform our thinking and our social systems. Dialogue, deliberation, and other powerful forms of conversation have a tremendous role to play in that. Conversation is the primary way we humans engage in conscious collective transformation—replacing the other primary way: violence and domination. That's the road out. And the kinds of collective breakthroughs that are possible through high quality conversation look an awful lot like the raw materials for conscious evolutionary leaps.

The conversational nature of evolution

So we need conversation for human evolution. But there's a bigger picture. As science writer Connie Barlow says, "The best metaphor I have found to describe evolution is this: conversation. Evolution is like a big conversation." In fact, all the complex interactions of the natural universe are like a big conversation. In a sense, the conversations we humans have are simply extensions of this far vaster conversation that has been going on for billions of years.

A basic pattern we see over and over in the history of the universe is that diverse entities—living together in information-rich environments filled with challenge and support—tend to interact in ways that generate new patterns over time. Often those interactions lead these entities to form novel collective entities that interact at entirely new levels. As the Great Story of evolution proceeds, this coming together and interacting in new forms becomes more inclusive, complex, and sophisticated.

This particular process started more than 10 billion years ago as vast clouds of invisible hydrogen gas coalesced into starless galaxies within which gravitational interactions gave sudden birth to stars, which lit up the void. From that point, stars were home to powerfully interactive forces that have continuously brought forth the chemicals that are the building blocks of planets and life. In the primal Earth's information-rich environments filled with challenges and supports, some of those chemicals became cells, which joined together into more complex cells (an evolutionary leap enabled by Earth's first and worst pollution crisis—the oxygenation of the atmosphere), and soon those cells formed colonies that developed into multicellular organisms—and those evolved into swarming ecosystems and wave after wave of new varieties of plants and animals. In each wave, some new, remarkable way of being together showed up.

Interaction, at its best, is both challenging and supportive

Any careful review of the evolutionary story reveals this direction—towards increasingly inclusive and complex cooperative arrangements in which the participating life forms live or die, succeed or fail, together. That process has continued right into the evolution of human culture, with cooperation happening first at family and clan levels, then tribes and local empires, and then countries and global corporations, organizations, and networks. We face the challenge today of crafting increasingly inclusive, sophisticated and wise worldwide cooperative systems, because it is becoming increasingly clear that we are all going to make it or crash together as a planet.

So evolution is a form of conversation—and conversation is a form of evolution. I mentioned the pattern of diverse entities changing because they interact in an information-rich environment filled with challenges and supports. That describes us, walking/talking our way towards becoming a branch of evolution that is—newly and powerfully—conscious of itself.

E-volve comes from "to roll out". *Con-verse* comes from "to turn together." We can rightly say that—as we turn together in conversation, we become the evolution we've been waiting for.

Responsiveness, fitness and intelligence

Underlying both evolution and conversation is intelligence—responsiveness to circumstances—the ability to observe what's going on, sort it out usefully and, based on that, behave appropriately for the circumstances. Organisms evolve because their environment has changed: Those that don't adapt get selected out, leaving behind whoever managed to succeed in the new environment. This is a rough but extremely workable form of intelligence, of finding out what works—at least at the collective level (it is often pretty harsh on individuals!).

Conversational evolution is more subtle and less dire: In high quality conversation, our ideas, our relationships, our feelings, our sense of possibility can all shift because we see things differently after talking with people who are different from us. If our differences reflect the diversity involved in the system or situation we are talking about, then the shifts we make reflect the complex realities we face.

This enables us to create new understandings and options that actually make deeper, broader sense. Together we are able to respond to the crises we face with greater comprehension, wisdom, and shared resourcefulness.

This is exactly what is needed to address the evolutionary challenges we face as a civilization.

So conscious evolution is a conscious search for—and adoption of—wiser forms of fitness in a changing environment. What is going on in that search for fitness?

Some dynamics in the search for fitness

There are three modes of interacting with our environment that add up to fitness, each of which makes sense in different circumstances. These are novelty, maintenance, and incremental improvement. I will explore them below—and also the role of intelligence as a guide for the search, and the role of community and awareness as two vital supports for all three modes in human systems. For all six of these factors, I will offer a few processes and practices that exemplify or further them.

NOVELTY/CREATIVITY. Many people think this is what evolution is all about. This mode of engagement involves newness and the bringing forth of newness. It includes innovation, originality, breakthrough, emergence, and exciting stimulation of all kinds. However, it may

Disturbance also be associated with uncertainty, risk,
tells us it is unfamiliarity, disturbance, chaos, and dissonance. In extreme cases, it involves the
time to get discontinuities of crisis, catastrophe, and
creative breakdown caused by the appearance of a challenge for which we are unprepared and thus clears the way (often painfully) for a new order.

Novel, creative dynamics are especially appropriate when the environment (including our internal environment!) changes rapidly and requires rapid changes in our own life patterns to maintain our "fit". Creative chaos laps at the shores of all systems, tossing novel developments and challenges into life whether or not it fits the needs of the systems involved. As long as a system is healthy and adaptable, it can successfully ignore these challenges—at least for a while. But when the system starts to malfunction, the more it resists change, the more insistent and successful the creative challenges become.

Some of the processes and practices that evoke deeply creative responses to life include transformational mediation, choice creating (associated with Dynamic Facilitation), brainstorming, Presencing (pioneered by Otto Scharmer, and its companion practice of "listening into the middle"), and Appreciative Inquiry. Also processes that work with "edges" (like Arnold Mindell's Process Worldwork) or that explicitly engage "The Other" (like diversity dialogues) or "welcome the stranger" (like Open Space) present a level of challenge that invites the emergence of new understandings, relationships, and possibilities.

STABILITY/MAINTENANCE. The evolutionary heart of this mode of engagement is *survival*. This mode focuses on conserving, adjusting, maintaining order or health, staying the course or getting back on course, and maintaining a level of predictability. This is the essence of sustainability, being able to maintain some kind of continuity. While at first, many people interested in change may see stability as anathema, it is crucial to a healthy, sane existence. However challenging the circumstances, knowing the sun will rise in the morning and set in the evening, for example, allows for some predictability! Maintenance provides the order that balances—and resists— the chaos of creativity. "If it ain't broke, don't fix it!" Here we also find the dynamics of balance: If a factor shifts a bit too much in one direction, shift it back. Maintenance factors are intrinsic to any system's ability to sustain its identity and structure. If it didn't resist change it would dissolve. This dynamic tension between order and chaos is a constant factor in life. Their dance moves this way and that way, depending on circumstances, with the balancing dynamics attempting to keep the dance from going too far toward either extreme.

Conservative efforts to maintain order are especially appropriate when things are going well. "Don't change anything." What's going well, however, may look different to different people, or at different time scales. Often the effort to maintain order involves making things look better than they are, or ignoring or denying unsettling energies that are bubbling under the surface. The broader and deeper the state of wellness, the more appropriate are the stabilizing energies.

Some of the healthy processes and practices that help sustain what's working are shared purpose, trust-building, agreed-upon values, validation, training, discussion, negotiation, mediation, and deliberation. Suppression may also work, but only temporarily, and with some nasty side-effects that tend to lead to systemic breakdown if carried on too long.

INCREMENTAL IMPROVEMENT. Between maintaining stability and all-out breakthrough is the progressive journey of slow change, little enhancements and reforms, adding a few bells and whistles, building-on just enough improvement to keep stability fresh and the revolutionaries at bay. We all do this in our lives, and markets specialize in arguably progressive versions of it. Each slight improvement stands on the shoulders of the last.

Much of evolution actually happens through incremental change, punctuated by the extreme evolutionary leaps characterized by creative novelty. In today's society, an incredible amount of change happens—largely initiated by novel technologies—without constituting a revolution in the basic assumptions of the culture. However, biological and cultural evolution tells us that incremental changes in an isolated population can add up to total shift (e.g., the emergence of a new species or language) over time. As certain populations lag or surge ahead in financial wealth, in adopting new means of communication, or in recognizing emerging trends and technologies, they can become essentially isolated from one another, vastly speeding up major shifts and discontinuities in society.

Some of the processes that support incremental improvement are Quality Circles, performance rewards, deliberation, evaluation reviews, and the full range of problem-solving techniques.

INTELLIGENCE decides which of these three modes is appropriate at any given time. In groups, organizations, and societies, collective intelligence decides when and where creativity, problem-solving, and maintenance actions will most serve survival and success. The core of intelligence—both individual and collective—is the ability to respond, to learn, to do what's appropriate. After all, what we want is a productive fit with our environment; we want to respond in ways that make sense. When we respond in

Creative intelligence helps us navigate our fit at the edge of order and chaos

ways that don't make sense, we call it a mistake. If we continue to make mistakes, we call that stupidity. On the other hand, intelligence that is very broad, deep, far-seeing, nuanced, and appropriate for both current and long-term needs is called "wise".

As noted above, intelligence—responsiveness to circumstances—is common to both evolution and conversation. It is present in all of the above three dynamics whenever they are applied appropriately. To a certain extent, they can be applied from above and outside the situation at hand. But the more complex a situation or system is, the more advisable it becomes to access the intelligence that is intrinsic in the situation or system itself.

Processes and practices that are good for accessing the intelligence of the system—and therefore can be used to stimulate creativity, conservation, or incremental progress, as appropriate to the system—include whole-system approaches like Open Space, Future Search, and World Café, as well as deep interpersonal methods like Nonviolent Communication. To support the search for fitness in groups, organizations, and societies—that is, to support collective intelligence—we need awareness and community. At any given moment in any given situation both are present to some extent. With luck—and facilitation or outside wisdom—there will be enough collective intelligence to notice where more awareness and community are needed.

AWARENESS includes consciousness, knowledge, understanding, insight, self-awareness, systems thinking, wisdom and more. Generically, it means simply the ability to notice and be present with what is. More specifically, it can mean awareness *of* particular dynamics, facts, or realities, and intentions regarding them.

Evolutionarily, we see awareness beginning with the first cells that were sensitive to light, sound and chemicals in their environments. Awareness has expanded to include very sophisticated senses, instruments that extend those senses (e.g., telescopes and computers), and minds that can process it all into meaning. In spiritual terms, awareness reaches beyond our usual senses deep into the subtle dynamics that generate thoughts, feelings, and realities. Although over evolutionary time more diverse modes of awareness have shown up, the most important evolutionary truth about awareness is that it needs to be appropriate to our needs, helping us respond. Yet sometimes awareness can overwhelm our ability to respond. Part of our evolutionary challenge is to expand both our awareness *and* our ability to respond—including greater tolerance of chaos, uncertainty, dissonance, etc.—i.e., capacitance—to just *be* with what is, so that appropriate responses can surface at the appropriate time. In evolutionary terms, as we increase our intimacy with evolution, we move from evolutionary awareness into the evolutionary flow.

Some of the processes and practices that can enhance different kinds of awareness include systems thinking, Bohm Dialogue, T-Groups, meditation, therapeutic dialogue, diversity dialogues, journaling, knowledge systems (often online), ritual, market research, and education.

COMMUNITY is the invisible web that binds us together. As our current social system has caused us to fragment into many disparate, self-interested subcultures, this web of connection has largely dissolved. Through conversation, we are beginning to consciously re-weave the web, bringing it radiantly to light. We are doing this through mindful, inclusive conversations such that the actual and perceived coherence and connectivity of human collectives consciously come together without loss of precious individuality and diversity.

Community is the human form of what emergence theorist Peggy Holman calls "differentiated wholeness." To have conscious collective intelligence we need

Evolutionary activists use high quality strategic conversation to jump-start collective intelligence

to both be uniquely ourselves *and* aware of ourselves as a collective, sustaining our collective being through the aliveness of our shared bonds and purposes. Community involves the vulnerability that opens us to one another, and the safety to translate that vulnerability into trust. It also involves various forms of common ground—shared language, culture, experience, tolerance, intentions, decision-making processes—even as it leaves

enough space for dissonance to allow for our differences and for the emergence of challenges and novelty when needed.

Among the processes and practices that serve community-building are story-sharing, networking, study circles, diversity dialogues, council circle, ritual, and visioning.

Conclusion

Now that it is obvious to many of us that today's trajectory of unconscious evolution is taking us straight towards a precipice of catastrophe and possible extinction, we might with good reason orient ourselves towards conscious evolution. That evolution will involve (and is involving) the transformation of our consciousness and our social systems—each of which profoundly affects the other, making both good starting points for change.

Wherever we begin, conversation is an essential strategic resource, given its powerful role as a catalyst for conscious co-evolution. This fact is especially important because crises set the stage for rapid evolution—and we will soon have an abundance of crises. Since we need a healthy dose of rapid evolution soon, our immediate future seems rich with opportunities to apply our collective consciousness and intelligence to transforming our world in high quality conversation.

We know that we need processes that help us sustain ourselves and succeed as we work to preserve and reform our lives and institutions. But in times like these, we most urgently need processes which draw out the creative initiative, collective intelligence and wisdom latent in our groups, organizations, communities, and whole societies—to say nothing of worldwide networks and beyond. We have such processes, we are rapidly creating more, and *we urgently need more focused research and development in this area, for we need even more powerful conversational wisdom. Our conversational approaches themselves need to consciously evolve.*

Who needs to talk to whom about what, in what way, for breakthroughs to occur? This is a question we can use to convene strategic evolutionary conversations and to guide research. Pursuing this inquiry can help us make a gentle, powerful difference at every level, in every sector.

Ultimately, if we make a good habit of all this, as a worldwide culture, we can become the first consciously evolving civilization in history—not bad for a species that looked like it was on the way out with a bang, fire and ice.

The Facilitator

The facilitator has no agenda
except the emergent agenda seeking to be born
in, among and through the people gathered before her.

Her emptiness is not nothing, though.
It is an invitation and a reflection.
Wherever she moves, radiating welcome,
things take shape, evolve, transform, move on.

She is delighted, fascinated,
    and as impartial as the Sun.
She offers comradeship on a journey
    into an open space
where co-creativity finds its home and voice.

The greater her skill, the less she does,
but the more profound the life she meets
because life loves, above all things, to find itself
and it always comes to where it can meet,
    embrace, and discover Greater Life,
which it finds in the universal center
    where she stands.

"Under the best of circumstances,"
    writes Harrison Owen,
"the facilitator will be totally present
    and absolutely invisible."

Like God. Like the Tao.
Like the Center of the Universe.
Everywhere—especially Here.

| ✳ |

Chapter Thirteen

Transformational leverage

Note that "leverage" is a linear, mechanical term. Some say it is an inappropriate concept to apply to a nonlinear complex living system like a society. Perhaps a term like "transformational sweet spot" or "butterfly acupuncture point" might be better. The point is that there are some realms in which a limited intervention is likely to have a bigger, more desirable, or more elegant impact than in others. I use "leverage" here because it is common parlance. Feel free to replace it with whatever term communicates comparable meaning for you and your audiences.

Not all activities, strategies, or activist groups offer the same capacity for social change, transformation, and evolution. The search for creating "more bang for the buck" is the search for leverage. Here are thoughts on what constitutes high and low transformational or evolutionary leverage. This is a narrative summary of a more detailed outline you can explore in Appendix C, if you wish.

High leverage

A basic understanding underlies the leverage perspective appropriate to the evolutionary activism explored in this book: If we want to have the most impact, we need to address the systems, patterns and technologies that generate what's healthy and unhealthy in our lives and our world.

We need to address societies' ways of operating. Ultimately the goal of evolutionary activism isn't to force people to do this or that, but to set things up so that society naturally and readily organizes itself in sustainable, healthy, beneficial ways. Some people call this approach "societal capacity building." It paints an elegant, efficient and holistic[5] path to a new civilization. That's good to have, even if our efforts in that direction may be quite bumpy and complex in actual practice.

Among the most powerful evolutionary interventions are those that enhance society's capacity to deal well with its public affairs and to pursue shared aspirations. We might ask, for example, "How does this society's way of making decisions help or hinder it in addressing what's actually going

---

[5] In this book *holistic* refers to a mindset or approach that embraces any or all of the phenomena associated with the term *wholeness* (see Appendix A), including diversity, multi-level phenomena, systems thinking, fractal dynamics, and complexity. Being fundamentally inclusive, it takes into account micro-level and individual phenomena covered by approaches often referred to as *reductionist*.

on?" Is there good information available? Is there a smart balance of roles among citizens, stakeholders, experts, and policy-makers in public decision-making? Is public attention being freed from addictive consumerism, lack of time, enervating entertainment, and complaints about problems? Is it being drawn toward engagement with meaningful activities, viable solutions and exciting possibilities? Often the quality of people's relationships, communities, and conversations provide important starting places in addressing these things, as well as transforming the actual institutions of governance and politics. Related to this, technologies that make people's interactions easier or more productive may have a significant impact when applied to public issues.

High leverage actions build society's capacity to maintain its fit with changing circumstances

Addressing the way the economy is set up also provides high leverage. Economies that undermine the health of human and natural communities do this so effectively because they are set up so producers, consumers, investors, and policy-makers can ignore those impacts. Green economists talk about "internalizing the costs", that is, making sure the costs of dealing with social and environmental harms are included in the price of harmful products and services. By adjusting our accounting practices and measures of corporate success, we can make it so the market automatically motivates producers, consumers, investors and policy-makers to make less harmful choices.

Another approach: Having more economic power and activity decentralized, local, and/or immaterial (like trading culture and information more than cars and caviar) helps reduce the transportation and material-use impacts of a global economy, while tightening the feedback loops that keep things in balance.

In order to make these shifts in governance and economic systems, we often need new technologies—social technologies, energy technologies, production technologies, digital technologies, and more. Many historians point out the leading role played by past innovations in transforming societies. Depending on the technology, this can be very high leverage indeed.

Of course, the way most people think about things also profoundly shapes society's ability to behave and respond well. So we could ask, "What new cultural stories and assumptions would make for a better society, and how might those stories and ideas best be spread?" Or we could bring more systems thinking and ecological and evolutionary awareness into schools and official deliberations. Or perhaps it would be better to promote them through YouTube and Twitter...

A final high-leverage intervention I want to mention is increasing the social, informational, organizational, networking and financial resources available to those doing evolutionary work. Given the high concentration of wealth in many societies, the transformation of philanthropy is a very high leverage project. This articulation of leverage, itself, arose out of an effort to bring these transformational issues to the attention of more philanthropists and social entrepreneurs, to help them expand their sense of what constitutes impact.

And although virtually every high-leverage approach described here already has advanced initiatives ready to promote, they also are only the beginning of what's needed. We are, as I often say, at Kitty Hawk in our transformational capacities. We can get our plane down the beach, but we're a far shot from the capacity we need for global jet travel—or rather, the conscious evolution of global civilization. We need more learning communities of practitioners and more research in virtually every area. Collective learning and research are central to the developmental process that *is* conscious evolutionary activism.

Understanding lower leverage

The more we have to push and pull people and organizations to do what's needed—for example with regulations—the lower the leverage, compared to setting things up so that people want to—or naturally—behave in appropriate ways. Rewards do better than punishments. But often what's most effective is showing them how what *they* most want can best be gotten by acting in this or that positive way. Many approaches to this exist. Reframing, public conversations, stories, peer networking, and social support can all tap into people's deeper desires and help them move away from dysfunctional behaviors. Campaigns based on these principles have helped people quit smoking, stop spousal abuse, lower carbon footprint and end child malnutrition, just to name a few.

We get less leverage from changing leaders and power-holders, whether by punishing abusers of power or voting great new politicians into elected office.

Unless we change the systems through which such people acquire their power or are elected to office—and the systems used to guide them once they are in power—the "good" ones may not show the promise we'd hoped for and can subsequently be replaced by even more problematic people who then go about their business at our expense.

Upstream action means changing **the factors that generate** *undesirable conditions*

Again, our search for leverage drives us towards changing systems.

Even lower leverage comes with our efforts to deal directly with the immediate problems associated with public issues. We can help the poor or clean up toxic dumps, which can be incredibly rewarding to both us and those individuals helped, but if more people are being driven into poverty or more toxics are being dumped, it will be a losing battle. The same goes for stopping wars or carbon emissions. As important as such actions are, sooner or later we need to face the fact that the more resources we invest in addressing the symptoms, the less resources we will have available to address the causes. This unfortunate reality only gets more intense the more symptoms show up. As more suffering, destruction, death, and catastrophe get generated, we naturally feel called to put our attention on them instead of dealing with the invisible systems and stories that make such horrors an increasingly painful presence in our lives.

As evolutionary activists we notice how our attention gets drawn toward immediate and painful symptoms—towards suffering and crises. This is natural; this is what evolution has prepared us to do. But we realize we need to be part of an evolutionary leap that takes us upstream beyond compulsive reaction to immediate suffering and danger. So we channel more and more of our attention to the systemic and cultural causes of what's happening, and to new patterns that could produce cascading benefits instead of harms.

(I admit one exception to this principle—that some threats are arguably so globally destructive that at least some evolutionary activists must take action to stop or mitigate them or else lose the runway needed to bring about the evolutionary transition we aim for. Still, efforts need to address causes as well as symptoms, horrifying as those symptoms may be. And to the extent we can focus on positive possibilities, we tap a powerful source of life energy.)

This approach of positive systemic change is not only ultimately more effective, it is more evolutionary. It follows a basic guidance covered further elsewhere in this book: For evolutionary activists, social problems, conflicts and crises are a resource, generating energy, opening dysfunctional structures to shift, and pointing towards needed systemic changes. Using society's issues and problems as guides to tell us what needs to be transformed can help us play effective roles in creating the new institutions, stories, technologies and worldviews needed to bring into being a sustainable global civilization.

Becoming wiser about leverage is critical to the success of evolutionary activism.

Life Like Spring

The spring shoots and buds
are uncertain
but they are coming up anyway
in many places
simultaneously.

They may yet
be blasted by frost,
but they are coming up anyway
in many places
simultaneously.

All we have
is each other
and our experience.
Talk to me.
The storm is here.
It is time.
We are coming up
everywhere simultaneously.

| ✳ |

Reflections on

Evolutionary Grace and

Appreciation

Chapter Fourteen

Goodness Gracious:
evolutionary integrity
and our engagement with life

Grace is the Goodness of Life. Grace is the impulse of Life and Reality to move from one state of wholeness to its next state of wholeness.

In one sense, Grace is always present, everywhere; it is how life works, how God or the Creative Power of the Universe moves, often "in mysterious ways". In another sense, Grace *happens*, sometimes manifesting when we call out for it, but often showing up serendipitously when we most need or least expect it, moving us to our next state of wholeness.

In still another sense, Grace is all the blessings—all the wholeness—that we ourselves can help bring into being through our good intentions and actions. And, in yet another sense, we can feel Grace moving us, using us and our circumstances to bring *itself* forth: In this state, we realize we are its vehicle, and it invites us to be mindful and grateful as we participate in its emergence, learning and awe-struck as we go.

Evolutionary integrity is our ongoing alignment with reality, becoming one with Grace

Evolutionary integrity, a close cousin of Grace, is the ongoing condition of being aligned with Reality in all its full-ness. And because Reality itself is al-ways changing, always moving to its next state of wholeness, evolutionary integrity is ultimately about our partici-pation in Grace—our active, blessed, and challenging role in the ever-emerging Goodness of Life.

Technically speaking, evolutionary integrity embodies the evolutionary dynamic of "fitness": It is about the ways Life fits—or seeks to fit—harmoniously and dynamically with What Is and What is Emerging. Evolutionary integrity is all about developing and maintaining our congruence with what is real and alive and arising—an ever-evolving congruence that allows us to survive, succeed, thrive, and be blessed by Life.

Spiritually speaking, evolutionary integrity is about serv-ing, manifesting, and becoming one with the Ultimate Crea-tive Power of the Universe in every aspect and moment of our unfolding lives. There is no distinction between us and the universal evolutionary process we see and are—except that it is way, way bigger than we are, as the ocean is bigger than the wave.

Central to evolutionary integrity is *appreciation*—right relationship with the Goodness of Life, with Grace, with the Ways Things Fit, and with our own best and sacred place in all that. Appreciation is all about how fully and sensitively we recognize and understand how the diverse manifestations of Life fit together, right here and now. It is about our own life-opening gratitude for Grace. It is about our active participation in bringing forth and increasing the value and impact of the Goodness of Life. Appreciation includes, ignites and reaches beyond mere noticing and action to fuel the energy of evolutionary integrity like cosmic reactors fuel the cores of every star.

Evolutionary integrity has four primary dimensions or manifestations—four ways to manifest and practice the power of active appreciation:

1. **BLESSING:** Appreciate the way you fit into life and the way life inhabits you and your world... the way you belong in Life—and in your particular life... Appreciate what is and has been good, comfortable, working, vibrant, enjoyable, and blessed in your life, in the person or situation in front of you, in your community and world. Hear, see and love the Life you encounter. Practices in this realm increase Trust, Joy, and Gratitude.

2. **GROUNDING:** Appreciate exactly who you are, what is happening and your role in it—and make it all available for

interactions in and around you. Seek to ground yourself thoroughly in the wholeness of dynamic Reality—in all its fullness, its vulnerability, its questioning—for that is the sacred space within which each new Goodness emerges, takes root, and evolves. Practices in this realm increase Authenticity, Humility, and Evolvability.

3. **VOCATION**: Appreciate where things could be better, where you feel drawn to bring forth more Goodness, where Grace calls you to act on behalf of Life and the evolution of its Goodness and Fit. The Goodness of Life includes the Goodness of our impulse to improve ourselves and our world, which guides our own conscious role—our calling, whether vocation or avocation—in the Great Story of Evolution. Practices in this realm increase Responsibility, Engagement, and Impact.

4. **INVOCATION**: Appreciate the promise of new Grace awaiting us on the other side of dissonance—through crisis and conflict, through problems and visions, through uncertainties and passions, through pain and alienation, through the voices of strangers and prophets. Call it forth!—for new Goodness wants to emerge through these throes of a sometimes messy birth. Invite it into being with your open intention, permission, support and encouragement, your ear and your heart, your patient, caring holding of space and time

for energy to flow so possibilities can unfold. Practices in this realm increase Service, Creation, and Transformation.

Practice these in your own self and life. Practice them in your relationships and community. Practice them through your citizenship, seeking to imbue emerging visions, cultures, social systems, tools, stories and consciousness with the appreciative power of evolutionary integrity.

A Powerful Grace

A powerful Grace
moves among us
and through everything,
the Source of the world
and of life that seeks life.

In every moment it is whole,
perfection inseparable
from its motion
into its next perfection—
each imperfection perfect
in its invocation of the next
perfect wholeness.

In and of the dynamic unfolding of wholeness
resides the Creative Grace of the universe,
driven from within from without,
eternally knitting The Fit
between like and unlike,
the dance of violence and brilliance and love
of which we are
in which we are
participants in Grace
awakening into

greater graceful grateful participation,
awakening to our part
in the coming and going
of wholeness,
of perfect Grace
now awake to Choice.

| ✳ |

Chapter Fifteen

Active appreciation

You aren't likely to be empowered by what you don't appreciate. —Michael Dowd

I have not usually considered *appreciation* a mode of social change activism. But I recently began to see it as having a multi-dimensional nature that could make it one of the most powerful approaches available to evolutionary activists. Its definition includes the following:

a. **liking, finding blessing in** - *appreciating the beauty of the sunset*

b. **gratitude for** - *appreciating the kindness of strangers*

c. **deep understanding** - *appreciating the difficulty of climbing the mountain*

d. **increase in value** - *their property kept appreciating as they completed home improvements*

So how is appreciation an approach to activism? I noticed a common thread running through many of the activist approaches I have been advocating for years: *Through noticing, believing in, or bringing attention to the (sometimes hidden) positive qualities or possibilities in a person or situation, we invite those qualities and possibilities to show up in the world more fully.*

I've begun to see this kind of active appreciation as a powerful form of nonlinear causation, a new approach to intentional action that's more aligned to what we've learned from chaos and complexity theories. *We don't have to MAKE something happen. We just need to help positive energies already present awaken and find channels to manifest in reality, following their own agendas. We don't have to input energy into the system; it's already there.*

When we use this approach, people tend to behave better and solutions and insights often show up as if by magic, often without even addressing a problem directly. Activists engaged in appreciative work tend to be more energized than those engaged in problem-solving and pushing solutions against the resistance of business as usual. They tend to burn out less than other activists, since they often gain more energy from their work than they expend.

So when we combine all four definitions of *appreciation* into one idea, featuring them together as a synergistic whole approach to action in the world, appreciation moves from being pretty passive to becoming a truly powerful concept. Like Gandhi did for *Truth* and King did for *Love*, we can do for *Appreciation*: Use its power to change the world.

Evolutionary activism is grounded in *evolutionary integrity*—right relationship with what is, or being aware of what's really involved and addressing situations creatively to preserve a healthy "fit" or move things on to a state of greater wholeness.

Use the positive aspects of what is to change the dysfunctional aspects of what is

In this light, active appreciation becomes an approach to practicing our activism with elegant evolutionary integrity—using the positive aspects of what is to change the dysfunctional aspects of what is. Active appreciation then becomes a conscious manifestation of the same creative dynamism that characterizes the Creative Power of the Universe that has driven evolution for billions of years.

Active appreciation as the central practice of activism with evolutionary integrity becomes something like

> *developing and using*
> *one's deep, engaged,*
> * Grace-filled understanding*
> *of a living entity, system, or situation*
> *to partner with it*
> *into fuller manifestations*
> *of its aliveness and evolutionary potential.*

Appreciation-based, integrity-motivated evolutionary activists would find themselves exercising attitudes like gratitude, empathy, and "crisis as opportunity"—and using tools like

- **Affirmation** - making statements of positive reality as if they are true in the present, awakening what is needed to make them real

- **The Pygmalion effect** - holding positive expectations of others to call forth the best in them

- **Appreciative Inquiry** - exploring what has worked and what we want in ways that inspire creative action now

- **Positive deviance** - finding out who in a system is addressing a problem well, and using them to help the system shift

- **Asset Based Community Development** - identifying all the possible gifts available from all the people and institutions in our community and helping them be available to meet community needs

- **Community Visioning** - a participatory effort to identify what our community wants to be like by a certain future time, and co-creating plans to achieve that

- **Callings** - seeing where our individual gifts and passions meet the needs of the world, and living lives that nurture that "sweet spot" of meaning and service

- **Backcasting / imagineering** - inviting people to imagine themselves in a positive future and "remember" how they got there, usually in an exercise or a work of fiction

- **Open Space** - a self-organizing conference to help us productively pursue our individual passions with others who share those passions

- **Nonviolent Communication** - exploring what we are each feeling and needing and finding ways to meet those needs in mutually satisfactory ways

- **World Café** - mix-and-match café "conversations that matter" around "questions with heart and meaning"

- **Strategic Questions** - powerful questions designed to stimulate positive change even when they are not answered, by reframing how we think about things

- **Dynamic Facilitation** - translating "impossible problems" into breakthroughs through reflective listening and exploration of possibilities

- **Focusing** - an inquiry into what's at the heart of a situation by inquiring into our "felt sense" about it

- **HSLing** ("hizzeling") - a compassion practice arising from the Dalai Lama's saying "When people don't feel Heard, Seen, or Loved, mischief occurs."

- **Pattern Languages** - mapping out interrelated design elements in a situation or practice that together generate wholeness, aliveness, and fit

These and many other active appreciation practices call forth or tap into the positive life-force—passions, dreams, successes, gifts, callings, energies, capacities, opportunities— in people, nature, and situations. They help us align living realities (including ourselves) into newly whole (healthy, sacred, vibrant, coherent) patterns of relationship.

This is the essence of evolutionary integrity and offers tremendously valuable tactical and strategic guidance for evolutionary activists.

The Whole Knows

The Whole knows us
better than we know ourselves.
and It sees Itself in each of us
and invites us to See, as well,
Itself deep in ourselves and one another.

The Whole evolves, unfolds,
through all Its manifold selves and interactions
and longs for its next Beingness
through us,
through our longing.

And the Whole dreams Itself
through our dreams,
and visits Itself in our visions.

The Whole invites us
into what's next,
invites us
into joining as partners
in the Whole unfolding Story.

The Whole loves our gifts and limitations,
our passions and our needs.
It calls us to Its service
through our gifts and passions —
guiding us through them
to our place
in the Whole unfolding Story.

And the Whole has a powerful purpose
for everything we lack:
It calls us to connection
to one another
and to Itself
through our limitations and our needs,
as the gifts of one
meet the needs and limitations of the other,
joining us all in a stream of evolving wholeness
flowing from lack to abundance,
carrying us through the gates of Hello.

The Whole is on the move
flowing through every detail of life.
Its current of life flows everywhere—
masquerading as us
giving, receiving, making, serving,
through me
through you
adventuring
through this day
as I write,
as you read,
inviting us
to wonder together
into a Whole new world
        forever.

| ✳ |

Reflections on

Crises and Democracy

Chapter Sixteen

Six degrees of separation
from reality

When you are standing on the edge of a cliff,
a step forward is not progress.

— Anonymous

In Juliet Eilperin's September 25, 2009 *Washington Post* article, "New Analysis Brings Dire Forecast of 6.3-Degree Temperature Increase", she describes UN-sponsored research into what will happen "by the end of the century even if the world's leaders fulfill their most ambitious climate pledges." It updates the 2007 report by the UN Intergovernmental Panel on Climate Change (IPCC) whose 2005 scientific foundations have been significantly transcended by more recent research which suggests climate change is progressing faster than the IPCC's worst-case scenarios. More research shows up each month pointing in the same direction, revealing new data on Arctic sea ice, glacial melting and movement, release of potent greenhouse gasses from the thawing tundra and undersea methane deposits, and other factors and feedback loops.

Surely some more intense efforts are called for. Before, during, and after every international gathering where agreements will be made that will make or break our climate future, we all need to deepen our understanding of the shifting realities we face and our commitment to changing them in more sustainable, wise directions.

Scientists are clearly doing their part in this, as are activists like 350.org and many artists and performers. I hope many more activists and artists will see how this issue connects to whatever issues they are working on. I hope journalists and academics will recognize the supremacy of this issue and sustain public and official attention on it, for the benefit of the whole society—the whole world. I hope that dialogue and deliberation practitioners will ask themselves and one another, "What conversations can we convene or facilitate which would make the biggest difference in this issue, given our current skills and connections?" I hope systems thinkers will help more people understand how both climate change *and* the various social forces that undermine our ability to address it are natural products of our current social systems— especially our economics and politics. I hope they help us see what changes could shift those systems into less self-destructive forms.

Above and beyond these hopes I see a pattern, an evolutionary dynamic at work. Evolution demands that we be aligned with reality as it really is. When any organism falls out of alignment—when it doesn't fit, when its ways don't work any more—reality steps in to correct the dissonance, one way or another. Organisms, ideas, governments, businesses and technologies die or go extinct while new ones or changed ones arise that are more in alignment with What Is.

Civilization cannot long continue as an exercise in being invulnerable to reality's limits

There are many ways to view our current civilization in this dynamic. One of them is that modern civilization is an exercise in making us invulnerable to the efforts of reality to limit or correct our behaviors, ideas, and systems. We don't let people die. We protect ourselves from weather and risk. We build bridges over rivers, cables under oceans, rockets through vast spaces. We create abstractions (like "powers of ten") that carry us far beyond what we can sense and thus respond to—or religious, political, and scientific ideologies that deny whatever contradicts them, whatever lies outside them. We flush our "waste" "away" (although neither concept has any reality in natural systems). Whenever nature intervenes and says to us "Don't Do That!", we take that as a problem to be solved—and measure our cleverness by our ability to keep doing that thing that got us in trouble. We rebuild on the floodplain. We fasten our seat belts. We buy more insurance. The higher or lower the temperature goes, the more we use our energy-intensive heating and air conditioning systems, emitting more CO_2 into a climbing climate. We just don't stop.

We are geniuses at impacting the world while preventing impact on ourselves. As we solve our lives into greater and greater separation from the built-in learning mechanisms of evolution, nature has to stretch further and further to heal itself, to get us to pay attention so that we stop treating feedback as a problem and see it as an increasingly urgent invitation—indeed a demand—to take notice and to change. Yet still we go further and further out on the limb, brilliantly resisting nature's limits and messages.

Our separation from nature—or should I say, our separation from reality as it really is, in all its fullness that is so hard for us to grasp—has now reached global proportions. Reality's feedback is now coming in the form of increasingly extreme weather, aquifers empty of water, oceans empty of fish, cancers arising from an environmental chemical soup so complex we can no longer track the causal links, new diseases that won't respond to antibiotics and can span continents and seas in hours on jets, and small groups and networks with increasingly powerful destructive technologies at their disposal.

We are rapidly moving into a realm where problem-solving becomes obsolete, if not downright dangerous, if we continue trying at all costs to preserve our systems, our habits, our identities, our protections and privileges. Today's biggest challenges are not primarily problems to be solved. They are realities to engage with, to come to terms with, to learn something from about who we are in the world, to be humbled by and creatively joined. Yes, joined. Because inside the realities of today are profound lessons about who we need to be next, individually and collectively—about the cultures, technologies, stories, and social systems we need to create and move into. We won't learn those lessons if we see these realities as merely problems to resist or resolve—or worse, to make another war on. We need to see them as embodying the precise information we most desperately need to take in right now.[6]

Six degrees of temperature rise. Six degrees of separation from one another. Six degrees of separation from reality. We need to find our way back, to find ways to be distinctly ourselves without losing our communion with the larger whole of Life. We need to creatively weave ourselves back into the feedback loops reality provides to keep the whole of Life healthy. We need to create newer forms, higher forms of answerability to reality—to question the role of insurance, of "limited liability corporations", of entertainment, of cost-benefit analyses, of efficiency, of everything that protects us from being with what's real here and now, from the consequences of our actions and from awareness of our changing world—indeed, from everything that helps us act as if we're separate.

Because we're not.

---

[6] I expect additional insights will come from exploring the relation ship between these ideas and the concept of *wicked problems* en.wikipedia.org/wiki/Wicked_problems.

Mother Earth's Message

I went to Mother Earth last night;
a tear within my eye.
I said I feared that she was through;
I asked her please what we could do
*   to make it   so she would never die.*
*   She shrugged   and asked me why.*
*   And then she said to me....*

She said
Don't you worry 'bout me, boy.
I' been 'round for billion years.
You humans, you just come and go
with all your mess and blessedness,
your shopping mall Apocalypses,
*   killing fields and beers,*
*   all your hopes and fears,*
*   all your dreams and tears....*

But I'm mom to more than you, boy.
I'm mom to life itself.
And me and life will still be here
if you're no more than a drying tear....
*   a trace   on nature's face*
*   that I'll somehow replace,*
*   replace with someone else*
*   my dear....*

So save your own sweet sassafras.
Save your home and town.
But while you do it, don't forget
that you are part of a living net
that gives you everything you get.
   And every time you cut another down,
   the spring it gets more tightly wound.
   Each cut will one day come around
      to you....

So don't you worry 'bout me, boy.
I' been 'round four billion years.
It's your soul you gotta look out for.
It's caught behind a closing door,
a heavy door of greed and fear,
of deadly smiling gold veneer.
   You're trapped within a room
   with the lives that you consume.
   You will know the timber's tears
   and the plans of profiteers.
   Do not shrink from what you hear
   or you shall disappear
      my dear.....

For as you prosper now, my boy,
you drag the others down:
the eagles and the antelope,
the dolphins and the buffalo,
the billions that you'll never know
in the falling jungle domino.
  The poisoned places grow,
  up above and down below....
  hurricane and undertow....
  the Storm begins to blow....
  Soon you'll have to go,   you know.....

There are so many of you, boy,
you've gotten out of hand.
You never stop when there's enough.
Each year you're into bigger stuff.
Your big boys like to play it rough.
  You're bulls in nature's shop.
  You know it's gonna stop.
  Your towers all will topple down
    on you.....

You see the end of everything,
I see the end of you.
The pity of it is that you
could be with me as I am with you

and see that I am always new
  and always very old...
  and always hot and cold...
  and always everything
    that sings....

So don't you worry 'bout me, boy.
I'm mom to life itself.
And me and life will still be here
if you're no more than a drying tear,
  a trace on nature's face
  that I'll somehow replace,
  replace with someone else...
  replace with someone else...
  There are so many more to come, my dear.....

I went to Mother Earth last night,
a tear within my eye.
I said I feared that she was through;
I asked her please what we could do
  to make it   so she would never die.
  She shrugged   and asked me why.
  And then she said to me....
        don't you worry 'bout me, boy.....

| ✳ |

Chapter Seventeen

Something bigger than Life is trying to work through us

More and more, I feel called to talk about crises, as creatively and usefully as I can.

Clearly crises are coming; some are very much here. Once reserved for the fringes, crisis talk has gone mainstream. We aren't talking "apocalyptic extremists" anymore. We're talking the respected chief economist of the International Energy Agency saying we'll be feeling serious economic impact from peak oil in the immediate future.[7] I wrote this essay immediately after four exhausting days of over 100 degree temperatures in my hometown of Eugene, Oregon—and new reports say that the humungous Greenland ice sheet is going to melt, regardless, more than doubling estimates of sea level rise.[8]

---

[7] tinyurl.com/nmemcg

[8] www.newsweek.com/id/208164

A scientist friend faulted me for having a few ounces of fish each day for breakfast—which I do for a cardiovascular condition—because the oceans are dying...[9]

We can no longer act as if such information is merely the hope-curdling pessimism of doom-and-gloomers. It is now our daily news. But listening to it presents a quandary: On the one hand, it feels increasingly odd to proceed with life as usual in the face of it. On the other hand, what exactly are we supposed to do about it?

The more I delve into the situations we face, the less I see clear or easy answers. However, in this challenging process I am coming to realize a few things.

One of the big ones: To the extent our anguish over the coming crises is a cry for no disruption in our lives—and that is certainly part of my own anguish—I suspect we will not find *any* answers, because our business as usual patterns are so closely tied to the destructive systems at work on our planet. Nothing we do to change our small lives within the business as usual systems will change that disturbing fact. Only changing those systems will.

But changing a system is a gigantic, long-term undertaking. More immediate issues confront us. For example: once we face the fact that business as usual is not an answer, a logical next step is to prepare. But...

---

[9] tinyurl.com/kk3lug

What does it mean to prepare?

I consider the options most often talked about in crisis-conscious preparation circles.

There is the option of personal material preparation—of stocking up, gardening, investing in gold, figuring out where to move, and so on. These are all useful as far as they go, but when we think them through, they just don't go far enough. Other people fleeing adjacent areas of hardship would likely seek security of their own in whatever island of security we've managed to create. If they are welcomed, they would likely overwhelm our supplies. If they are turned away, some will try to take what we have.

We can prepare our communities, but the same holds true there. I do believe that resilient sustainable communities are part of the future, and are a top priority for our creative energy (see Transition Towns[10]). But what about the community next door? What about the migrants from afar, whose lives have been shattered?

Nowadays it seems to me like there is nothing to prepare except the world. For most of us, that seems too big. (As bright spots on the horizon, however, Transition Towns and related initiatives are making a valiant attempt to do exactly that, from the ground up.)

Of course, to whatever degree we co-create our own suffering in our minds, we can do psycho-spiritual practices that enable us to experience disruption and pain without

---

[10] transitiontowns.org

actually experiencing much *suffering*. There are ample tools for that, from meditation to belief-changing practices.

Although such practices can help us productively engage with *whatever* happens, reliance on them can be part of separating ourselves from what is happening in the larger world and what it means for who we humans are together in the Great Story of Life. It can short-circuit our energy into a narrow narrative of personal salvation and away from larger efforts for a positive shift.

> *Crises are a sign that evolution is trying to break through a business as usual that isn't working*

In search of big-picture transformation

The above paragraphs explore the sort of thoughts that come to me when I think of saving me and mine. However, what energizes me—and it is a calling filled with struggles, aliveness, and the most remarkable people I've ever met—is to center my life on serving that transformation of the world that is crying to happen *through* the crises that are emerging around us.

When I look at the big picture, I get the sense that we are part of something larger that is "trying to happen." What I do with my life is a symptom, a sign of particular energies that are blowing in the wind. When I seek my own salvation—and extend it to everyone seeking their own salvation—

it seems to me a symptom of The Whole coming apart, breaking into fragments that think they can survive alone. When I seek the transformation of The Whole—the whole society, the whole culture, the whole world—it feels like a small manifestation of the whole of humanity seeking to heal into something new, feeling its way into a future that is more wholesome.

It feels like none of it is really about me. It is about the whole, the whole of life, the thrust and intelligence of evolution working its way through time, through me, through you, through us all and our world.

Being part of the Big Story

In these times of daunting emerging crises, some truths that most potently shape my life are these:

The Big Bang is our awesome primal ancestor. We are its children, its legacy. Its energy is ours, whether we know it or not.

We are the hydrogen dew of the Universal Beginning that was then forged in red giant stars and exploding supernovae to become every atom of our bodies and our world.

For billions of years, we've been flowing with every other particle in the universal river of stardust on an exquisite, unlikely, painful, magical, and infinitely creative Journey into the lives and worlds that we live in and are, today.

Over and over, I forget this awesome truth in my seemingly ordinary everyday life. Then over and over I remember it: Truly a miracle is unfolding within and around me, moment to moment, hidden by the camouflage of business as usual.

But for better and worse, you and I are on the verge of business as usual tearing itself apart before our very eyes, revealing the raw truth of evolution here and now in our time, in our place, in our hearts and minds. Evolution always speeds up in the verges, the edges, the crises, the between-worlds spaces where anything can happen....

And we, on that edge, are speeding toward a whole new identity, a whole new Story of who we are and what we are about.

Today we *are* the 13.7 billion year evolutionary adventure dreaming of becoming conscious of itself—of becoming knowingly choiceful—able to evolve by aware understanding, will, and caring. If we awaken, evolution will awaken, and we'll step consciously away from the cliff into a dramatically different, vibrant, co-creative world.

Crises are doorways that look like hurricanes

Hidden by our institutionalized not-see-ism, the crises that are coming are being co-created moment-to-moment by our collective consciousness, our technologies, our social systems, simply by doing what they were designed to do. These co-created crises are magnificent in their complexity, their challenge, and their perfect fit for our evolutionary awakening, which is underway even as you read this. They call us to look in the mirror of evolution and see ourselves clearly, to look at how we have set up our world. They call

Evolutionary activists know these crises are perfect for humanity's evolutionary awakening...

us to step out of the box—for the box is burning!—and to transform ourselves and our world by wise choice, creating the path as we walk it.

There is no waiting. There are no spectators. We are It. Our collective systems are what It is about, and we are All Doing It.

Our emerging crises are a call to become wiser, collectively—to become the deep collective wisdom and monumental creativity of evolution itself becoming conscious through us.

To become evolution is to see the vastness of the Story we are living, a Story of deep time stretching back through chains of shape-shifting ancestors—back through families, through tribes, through animals and plants... back, back through bacteria, molten Earth, stars, galaxies, elemental particles—back to the infinitely potent Great Radiance that birthed the universe as an Adventure, as a Family, as All Our Relations, as Us.

To become evolution is to realize that within the depths of the emergent Now reside the potent traces of Everything That Ever Was, shaping our next steps. Everything That Ever Was is within and around us, calling us urgently to awaken to what is trying to be born through us. Its Voice—the Voice of Tomorrow—the Voice of the Whole—is in every one of us.

To become evolution is to awaken and know in every cell that our still-adolescent human awareness, which arose out of evolution, is creating problems it cannot solve without transforming itself. It is to know that we, collectively, are *both* that adolescent awareness *and* its transformation.

To become evolution is to wake up to deeper and deeper awareness of our still-adolescent social systems—especially our political, governmental, economic, energy, technological, and information systems. All these systems arose out of evolution. They are now creating problems they cannot solve without transforming themselves and one another. To become evolution is to know that their systemic immaturity persists with our active participation and that *this* *.... if we use them wisely and compassionately for that purpose* *profound evolutionary moment* calls us to consciously transform our roles in those systems, to be conscious co-creators of them.

To become evolution is to wake up to the reality that we are co-evolutionary participants in everything alive and in control of nothing alive. To become evolution is thus to strive to learn how to be engaged, wise, creative awake partners *with* one another, *with* the world in which we live, and *with* the conditions of our time. Crisis is opportunity on the winds of dangers that can daze *or* awaken us. Crisis is the dangerous breaking of glass that opens locked windows of opportunity that require perceptiveness and courage to move through, with care.

To become evolution is to say "We are Life, I am Life itself, finding ways to live, ways that work for and nurture Life. This task is what Life is all about, now and forever. We are All. In This. Together."

Such big declarations, so much easier said than done. But such is the Story that makes meaning in my own life right now, in the midst of emerging crises. My efforts, your efforts, are part of the human story waking up to find its new proper place in the Universe Story. Our efforts are not about us. They are not even about winning or losing, succeeding or failing. They are about the great Unfolding, which we *are*.

A few guidances

For some years I have been passionate about exploring evolutionary dynamics that can be used to change social systems. In that exploration, Peggy Holman and I stumbled on the idea that evolution is about diverse entities interacting in nurturing and challenging contexts to create and sustain new forms of elegantly simple complexity. Each aspect of this definition now informs my life.

As evolution waking up...

- *I feel called to learn more about how to use our differences and our challenges creatively*, not simply as problems to avoid or solve, but as signs of new life pushing to emerge—and as invitations into a new, more whole tomorrow.

- *I feel called* to learn and practice potent forms of interaction—especially conversational and economic interactions—that nurture deep aliveness and lead to breakthrough. I feel called to notice—in my life and the
world—and to respond creatively to those interactions
that generate frustration, violence, and breakdown.

- *I feel called* to notice the role of contexts, and not take
them for granted. They so easily become invisible background, but they are *so* extremely important. For example: spaces, histories, intentions, worldviews, social systems, timing, the quality of conversation—all these are
potent contexts. They shape who and how we are and
what is possible. They offer "nonlinear leverage" for
evolutionary work. I feel called to attend to these and to
work with other evolutionaries to shape and weave
new contexts into a wisdom culture, mindful of their
power. The contexts we shape will shape what happens
to our children, to the Seventh Generation after them,
and to the children of all species.

- *I feel called* to seek the deepest, most elegant and inclusive simplicity on the other side of complexity. I see
that the shallow simplicities on this side of complexity—the oversimplifications that don't acknowledge,
welcome, and "digest" the full diversity and nuances
of who we are and what we face—are killing us and
our world. I dream of weaving ourselves into new
forms of alive organic complexity that are a simple,
straightforward joy to be dancing in...

Seek the elegant simplicity on the other side of complexity

I would not give a fig for the simplicity this side of complexity, but I would give my life for the simplicity on the other side of complexity.
— Oliver Wendell Holmes

Crisis invites us, then pushes us

I have seen all this over the last few years:

We are thoroughly dependent on systems that are destroying us and our world. The very designs and beliefs that make those systems powerful and toxic are the designs and beliefs that, once transformed, will make us new. "We have it in our power to begin the world over again," said Thomas Paine in another crisis era. "The birth of a new world is at hand."

I see clearly that the longer we delay needed changes, the more demanding they will become. The more we delay them, the fewer resources we will have to work with. The demands on our lives from these truths will become increasingly profound and revolutionary. Evolution, like water behind a dam, senses where all the cracks are, and is working on them right now with increasing intensity.

Not changing is not an option any more. How soon we consciously change—and how open we are to the Call of the Whole in and around us as we do it—will make the difference.

I have seen so clearly that all this is not about us as individuals.

It is not about
  issues and candidates.
It is not about
  good guys and bad guys.
It is about
  the larger motions
  we make together,
  and the cultures and systems
  that shape those motions.

Our individual suffering, our fear, our successes are meaningless transient eddies in the current of Life—unless they are part of shifting those larger motions, those cultures and systems, the Direction of the River.

The meaning of life—at least of my life—is increasingly tied to all this—to this waking into conscious evolution with others so that the Profound Possibility that is Larger than Life can happen through us with sacred beauty.

What is your role in this awakening
from our dream of business as usual
in Time,
so that the remarkable experiment
called human consciousness and civilization
will not vanish,
but thrive to greater heights,
and be a blessing for the world?

Prayer for Conscious Evolution

This is my small
offering to the storm of change
that is upon us

— that IS us ...

May it be increasingly
conscious of itself and
its creations.

May we all live
this dream
into Life

| ✳ |

Chapter Eighteen

Building wise democracy as crises emerge

Our democracy is in crisis, in a world of emerging crises. Our democratic institutions are not adequate to address rising challenges and looming catastrophes. Few citizens today would claim our system of governance is wisely addressing:

- social inequities and injustices
- environmental degradation and climate change
- technological dangers (including but not limited to increasingly available weapons of mass destruction)
- terrorism and extremism of all sorts
- the rising threat of global epidemics
- unsustainable, destructive economic activities
- the corruption of democracy itself

the list goes on and on....

These crises are interdependent, not isolated from one another. Like a hundred brooks and streams, they and other crises could converge into a raging torrent overflowing its banks and transforming the landscape of our lives and the prospects for our children.

In spite of this, our democratic institutions continue to promote:

    a. the relentless concentration of power which enables those in power to remove or bypass checks on power,

    b. the materialist culture orchestrated by that power and

    c. the systematic denial of the problems generated by (a) and (b).

Hard-fought battles and hard-won freedoms end up being co-opted by the materialist project. The power of labor is harnessed to negotiate pay raises, benefits and working conditions, instead of increasing our ability to control our own work lives and communities. The power of feminism fizzles into demands for equality in corporations, government and the military, rather than leading the transformation of society into a collaborative culture. "Labor-saving devices" increase the complexity, pace and stress of our lives. "Liberation" mutates into equal access to the culture of materialism. Too many of us no longer strive for greater humanity, joy and meaning in life. We settle for respectable, comfortable roles in our system's profitable degradation of what is truly precious.

Still, growing millions of us—each in our own way—feel that something is fundamentally wrong with the direction of our society. Most of us, though, can't quite give it the attention it seems to deserve, to sort it out and take effective action. It is so complex... and our daily lives absorb all our energy and attention, leaving us with only a haunting wish that something could be done about it. This testifies to the awesome power of our culture to distract so many of us from the ultimate essentials of life, even the survival of our own children and the natural world upon which the children of all species depend.

We need to change the character of democracy, and we need to do it soon. We need to make it wise.

Perhaps the darkest irony is that democracy itself has been transformed from the crown jewel of The Enlightenment into one of the most effective and insidious tools used by Power to manipulate us, the citizenry, the electorate, The People.

From manipulated elections and warped political deliberations to the use of the Bill of Rights to protect and empower "corporate personhood" ... from the usurpation of citizen power by faceless international trade bureaucrats to the propaganda-laden entertainments of our mass media ... from the reprogramming of citizens to think like "consumers" to the near-universal complaint of "What can one person do?" ... democracy has lost both its integrity and its potency. It does little now but strut about amidst media-supported pretense and illusion that fool fewer and fewer of the world's citizens every year. It would be pathetic if it weren't

so dangerous. We can't afford to have such obliviousness at
the helm of a civilization heading into the great storms already visible on the horizon.

We need to change the character of democracy, and we
need to do it soon. If we are to meet the challenges of the
21st century, we need to make democracy not only more
functional, but truly wise.

I realize the terms "wise" and "democracy" are not often
seen together. We have often heard of wise leaders—and we
will surely need such leaders. But if we put all our eggs into
that basket, there is a good chance we'll lose our democracy
and, with it, the wise, responsible leadership we were hop-
ing for. The concentrated power we give to leaders almost
always corrupts them. Ultimately, the problems of our collective fate always come back to us. Always, that is, if we
want to keep our democracy.

Catastrophe and hardship have throughout history been
used as reasons to concentrate power, to grab the reins, to
turn over sovereignty to The Man Who Can Make The Trains
Run On Time—the Hitlers and the Mussolinis. Beyond that,
with current and emerging enhancements of concentrated
political and military power, if we lose what democracy we
have, we may never get it back.

In summary: a democracy that is not wise will not be
able to handle the crises already emerging around us, and
will be lost.

So now is the time—while the worst of the coming catastrophes are still over the horizon (though visible to the far
sighted)—to create a democracy that is wise enough to sur-

vive and thrive in the Era of Consequences we are entering. We have resources right now to do it, if we choose to channel them into activities that will serve us in this historic effort.

There may be more political space to work in than we have previously thought. As existing systems become more unmanageable, those involved with them, including their leaders, are increasingly searching for alternatives. Wherever that happens, evolutionary opportunities open up. Breakthroughs can happen when such opportunities are taken before the clamor for oversimplified, strong leadership overwhelms our yearning to direct our collective fate with our own collective common sense.

As systems become unmanageable, people increasingly search for alternatives, creating openings for change

New possibilities open when we apply the co-intelligence perspective to the realm of politics. In particular, certain co-intelligent public conversations can provide us with seeds and building blocks for the wise democracy we need. Most people have not experienced conversations like this. However, properly designed, carried out, and embedded in the political system, these conversations would transform ordinary, isolated citizens into an unlimited source of collective intelligence, wisdom and democratic guidance for the times ahead.

If we're going to turn to leaders, let us look for servant leaders who will make it possible for We the People to powerfully and brilliantly lead ourselves.

Integral Deliberative Democracy

This vision of wise democracy is also called "integral deliberative democracy."

- It is *integral* because it combines many co-intelligent approaches into a conversational loom upon which we can weave our diverse perspectives—even polarized views—about public issues into public wisdom and will. Gathering our differences like strands of multicolored yarn, it brings forth more inclusive ways of understanding our world and one another for mutual benefit.

- It is *deliberative* because it achieves this integration not through ivory tower model-making or dictatorial force, but by respectful, creative conversation among diverse ordinary people who truly hear one another, learn where their diverse gifts fit into a larger whole, and find themselves changing together in the process, connecting more deeply with themselves, with one another, with more of what is real, and with their common interests and dreams.

- It is *democracy* because the whole system is designed to empower the best that We the People, collectively, have to offer. It is grounded in our potential for wisely guiding and co-creating

our collective affairs. Together we can be our own
wise sovereign, our own inspired leader.

Integral deliberative democracy includes our voting, but
it makes that basic democratic activity more meaningful and
effective by creating space for better choices to emerge and
then deepening our understanding of them and the trade-
offs involved, expanding the wisdom of our choosing. And
then it does more, empowering us to envision and actually
build exciting common futures together. The trademark of
this new brand of democracy is groups of diverse citizens
deliberating on public problems and possibilities in ways—
and with powers—few of us have ever dreamed of.

The varieties of citizen deliberation

Sometimes these groups may comprise a dozen or so
citizens picked at random to express the feelings of an entire
population. Sometimes they may contain several dozen diverse stakeholders whose familiarity with a problem covers
all the major viewpoints involved. Sometimes hundreds or
thousands of citizens may be involved in study, dialogue,
analysis, evaluation and creativity around critical issues. They
may volunteer, be chosen by the conveners, or elected by
their fellow citizens.

Sometimes these citizens may focus on studying an issue.
Sometimes they may be voicing a range of public concerns
about the overall direction of their community or society.
Sometimes they may be envisioning possible futures—good

Temporary panels of ordinary citizens, given adequate information and support, can make citizenship into a laser of democracy

and bad—dreaming together or tracking trends or probable consequences. Sometimes they might be examining the performance of candidates or officeholders, or monitoring the progress of a governmental program or the ethical operations of a corporation. They may be reviewing laws that have already been passed, or they may be commenting on new ballot initiatives proposed by nonprofit groups, corporate lawyers, legislators—or other citizen panels.

There is no limit to the kinds of panels or uses to which co-intelligent citizen panels can be put. We're not talking about the all-too-familiar and torturous "committee meetings" and "public hearings," but rather about deep, authentic, no-holds-barred conversations that are designed (and usually facilitated) to get at the heart of the matter and to evoke the best that the participants have to offer. This is a totally unprecedented vision of democracy. Not only is it more potent and potentially wise than the down-home vision of town hall democracy, it is more scalable: We can establish viable integral deliberative democracy in cities and countries with millions of people.

Most of the conversations that make up an integral deliberative democracy happen all over the society—in homes and churches, in workplaces and libraries, in bars and cafes and classrooms—in a thousand different forms—generating a truly informed and engaged population. However, integral deliberative democracy is particularly marked by key conversations of selected (often randomly selected) citizens who, as temporary deliberative councils, perform various higher functions in the political process, including informing all the other conversations going on.

These ordinary citizens—who embody but do not "politically represent" the diversity of their communities—carry out powerful, official deliberations ordinarily reserved for think tanks and legislatures. They tap into the expertise around them, becoming expert themselves. However, unlike most think tanks and legislatures, these citizen councils bring a first-hand sense of their communities' values and a common sense appreciation of how the issues they're studying impact ordinary people like themselves. They do not live in ivory towers. They are not millionaire lawyer politicians. They are us, The People.

But they are not *just* The People. They are The People informed and engaged, a rich diversity in search of a wise consensus. Their conclusions are not the sort that one finds in most opinion polls and election tabulations. Given the time, information and facilitation to delve deeply into all sides of an issue, these folks are less susceptible to propaganda. Often they know more about a subject than the legislators who are voting on it in the congresses and parliaments of the world, or overwhelmed citizens beset by confusing interest group claims and emotional imagery. Furthermore, as ad hoc groups convened for a few days or weeks or months, they are (like juries) much more immune to pressure than standing bodies of professional politicians and bureaucrats.

These citizen deliberative councils use leading-edge group processes, facilitation, and sometimes advanced information and communications technologies to do their research and dialogue—and sometimes they even cross-examine leading experts and officials. Such resources *and time* are not available to most of us—a fact which makes it hard for most of us to make sense of all the dozens of complex issues we are called to comment or vote on. The complexity of the issues we face and the busy-ness of our lives make it almost impossible to exercise our *individual* citizenship wisely. However, we can *collectively* make precious communication and informational resources available to small, officially-convened, randomly selected groups of us, to think and act on our behalf and to inform us when they've gotten a handle on what should be done. In this way, we can make our citizenship meaningful once again—as a whole society—without all of us having to get involved in endless meetings ourselves.

Because they are specially chosen, facilitated, and empowered to learn, these citizen councils are able to go deeper and wider and higher than most of us can. They are more able to see The Big Picture, to find meaningful common ground among diverse perspectives, and to craft truly wise recommendations for policy and action. Wisdom is, after all, big-picture intelligence, applied to the real situations we're involved in.

An inclusive evolutionary adventure

This exciting new direction for politics does not replace adversarial debate and power politics. Rather, it contains them, and uses them for its own purpose: the enhancement of the common good. Because it uses co-intelligent processes, it can encourage both unity and diversity, agreement and dissent, since both are valuable resources for realizing the common good. It doesn't demand or require mass participation, but empowers those who want to participate to do so in more meaningful, effective ways. Above all, it taps the unrealized power of ordinary people to generate the collective wisdom we need to navigate the rough waters ahead.

Co-intelligent processes recruit both unity and diversity— both agreement and dissent— to serve the common good

Furthermore, if, in time, those waters grow calmer and less dangerous—as indeed they should if we address our problems with real wisdom—integral deliberative democracy offers us a path to continually realize new collective visions and co-create better futures together. Whatever society we want, this is a powerful tool for getting there. Not only can we use it to make our lives better, but also to pursue our development as a civilization evolving consciously, on an ongoing basis.

Those who want a healed natural world can use this tool to get it. Those who want a society that promotes individual and group development can use this tool to create such a society. Those who want more time, or more peace, or more justice, or more care for our children, or more beauty in our cities, or more sustainable economies—in short, anything that serves the common good—can use integral deliberative democracy to further those goals.

This is all possible because ordinary people, when they have the full information, when they have access to one another's perspectives in a creative, respectful setting, when they are fully heard and challenged to rise to the occasion on behalf of their whole community or country or world, will gravitate towards what is most deeply important to most people. It is natural. It has been demonstrated.[11] It is almost inevitable. As long as we empower them to do it.

Those, on the other hand, who want to arrange things for their own benefit at the expense of the lives, communities, nature, beauty, meaning, and spirit of others, will find that integral deliberative democracy frustrates them at every turn. If the system is designed correctly, they will find few avenues to mold the minds of these free, creative groups acting on behalf of their fellows and a healthy future.

This is not to say that everything will be perfect or that every decision of such citizen councils will satisfy all of us. "Perfection" is an irrelevant distraction. The important thing is to be able to learn—and apply what we learn—from wher-

---

[11]   See, for example, Chapter 13 of my book *The Tao of Democracy*, "Citizens Deliberate about Public Issues" online at bit.ly/3q2PKJ

ever we start.[12] I believe that the wisdom created in co-intelligent conversations by ordinary members of a community is the highest wisdom that that community as a whole is ready to hear and ready to live. It is appropriate, useful wisdom—a dependable starting place for the learning that will happen next. Since it will not be perfect wisdom (no wisdom is), the imperfections will show up, to be explored in broad public conversation and by subsequent citizen councils—again hearing many viewpoints—and worked over into something even wiser.

This is important, especially for both the utopians and the cynics among us. Integral deliberative democracy doesn't create some ideal state and stop there. It is a process, not a destination. It helps us create better wisdom and better social conditions each time around, learning as we go. It is a way of creating our lives well together, over and over, forever. It is a way of consciously evolving, together, as a global

---

[12] A most important topic to attend to if we wish to institutionalize citizen deliberative councils into our political and governance structures is preventing corruption of this new approach as it is adopted. Historically, every democratic innovation has been co-opted, corrupted, or undermined by special interests. This will be no exception. As Wendell Phillips reminded us over 150 years ago, "Eternal vigilance is the price of liberty—power is ever stealing from the many to the few." Particularly vulnerable are the quality of information and facilitation, which perhaps would best be overseen by an organization of prior participants in citizen panels. In any case, the systems set up for oversight will be key, and can be guided by our growing awareness of feedback and collective intelligence, as well as of evolutionary dynamics. We need to set effective precedents in the early stages before widespread visibility or adoption.

culture, within and among our diverse local and group cultures.

It is a way of finding better paths, and being empowered to take those paths, whenever the time is ripe or the need urgent.

All this is not part of any finalized blueprint. It is an opening into new possibilities, the start of an adventure. Many different techniques, approaches, visions and understandings already exist around us and among us as resources for building the kind of political culture we need. The co-intelligence perspective provides a sense of how we might fit all these pieces together into coherent systems that can be more powerful than their parts. What we each currently view as our methodology, our profession, our life, is in fact a strand of a mythic emerging fabric. It is waiting to be taken up—by ourselves and one another—as part of a larger emerging pattern of possibility we will weave into hopeful, life-serving futures for our world.

I hope you can "smell the bakery around the corner" as vividly as I can. I hope your mouth waters, your stomach grumbles, and your visionary appetite expands—as mine does—at the enticing possibilities so close, awaiting our eager arrival...

If enough people smell this bakery, we can be assured there will be bread for all.

We are on the edge

We are on the edge
very high up
and the fog has moved in.

When you are on the edge
very high up
and the fog moves in
  you need to be very alert
    and stand very still.

If you must move,
  you need to move back from the edge
    very carefully
    knowing each foot is on solid ground
    before putting your weight on it.

We are on the edge
very high up
and the fog has moved in.

The fact that our feet are on solid ground now
does not mean
that our feet will be on solid ground in our next step.

Stop.
This is not a time for mistakes.
It is not a time for progress.
It is not a time for business as usual.

What time we have
is for paying attention.

| ❋ |

Chapter Nineteen

Democracy and the evolution of societal intelligence

Have you ever been in a stupid group made up of intelligent people? I mean, each person in the group is pretty smart and creative, but when they get together they seem to get in one another's way? They can't seem to make decisions, they fight, they can't get things done. Or maybe they make decisions that are unimaginative—or even destructive. Or they just go round and round as the world passes them by.

Or maybe the groups you know have a strong leader. If the leader is good, maybe the group acts intelligently—makes good decisions, gets things done. But maybe the leader is bad... or maybe people are rebelling against a good or so-so leader... or maybe a good leader burns out and the group flounders.

Or maybe some group you know has a unifying ideology or belief that holds them all together—until someone tries to do something creative or different...

Have you experienced these things? Have you ever seen them among activists in social change movements?

Societal intelligence is the ability of a society to engage successfully with changing circumstances

I have. And I've also experienced a few rare groups where everyone is a peer, where leadership is shared, where a special kind of energy among them allows them to explore and solve problems together, successfully. I've watched people with very different ideas, backgrounds, aptitudes and knowledge using that diversity creatively. They come up with brilliant solutions and proposals—better than any of them could have come up with alone. The group seems more intelligent than its individual members.

Seeing these extremes, and observing what a large role these dynamics play in efforts to make a better world, I've chosen to study them, to see what I can learn.

I call these dynamics "collective intelligence"—which manifests as "group intelligence" in groups and "societal intelligence" in whole societies.

> *Intelligence refers to our ability to sort out our experience in ways that help us respond appropriately to circumstances—especially when we're faced with new situations.*

> *Societal intelligence, then, refers to the ability of a whole society to learn and cope creatively with its environment. Societal intelligence includes all the characteristics and institutions that help whole societies respond collectively and appropriately to their circumstances.*

Although I first got interested in this subject by observing dysfunctional activist groups, I soon realized that these groups simply manifested the dynamics of our dysfunctional society. Our society as a whole doesn't know how to solve its problems intelligently, doesn't know how to use its diversity creatively, and is moving inexorably towards its own self-destruction. Was it any wonder that many activist groups displayed the same characteristics?

It seemed to me almost axiomatic that, if we don't improve collective intelligence—our collective problem-solving, responsive capabilities—none of our other social and environmental problems would get solved. And, if we could achieve some breakthrough in societal intelligence, all the other problems would, in a sense, solve themselves in the natural course of socially-intelligent living. You don't have to solve all a person's problems for them if you increase their ability to solve their own problems. The same goes, I suspect, for societies.

So I've been doing some research on this. And one of the first things I stumbled across was the possibility that democracy is a stage in the evolution of societal intelligence.

Let's suppose societies go through stages.[13] In an early stage, a society might be run by the strongest warriors. Such a society would organize itself and survive through the use of physical force. Force has a black-and-white, win/lose logic to it which works in simple circumstances but doesn't work in the face of (and cannot support) greater complexity or subtlety. As the need for more complex relationships evolves, such a society should seek to complexify its repertoire of responses.

They might, let's suppose, shift into a stage where traditions are the guiding principle. Every problem has a standardized solution, handed down from generation to generation. Almost like instincts get handed down genetically, traditions are handed down through instruction and example. Traditions (like instincts) usually evolve from experience, so they're appropriate and workable as long as the environment doesn't change. But a society may find tradition hampers their creative responsiveness when they're faced with novel circumstances.

In a sense, a society based on ideology may be similar to one based on tradition. Ideologies are usually powerfully useful within a specific zone of operation. But they have their

---

[13] The "stages" view of development has tremendous gifts and limitations, with the limitations becoming more problematic the more we reify the stages in general terms, as I am doing here. I find the gifts of such models come to the fore to the extent we consider the stages as nonlinear and fractal, sometimes manifesting within one another at different scales of observation, sometimes going through iterative cycles in which they show up in new forms in new circumstances in a spiral of development. A "stage" becomes more like a useful pattern that tends to show up in a certain relationship to the other stages, but not always, and not always simply.

limits and, when those limits are reached, the ideology prevents successful, intelligent responses from emerging.

When traditions or ideologies are made obsolete by changing circumstances, a society needs to find a more flexible form
of intelligence. It needs to be able to observe changes, create
new appropriate responses, and then
implement those responses.

Societies seem to have different
strategies for this. The wise leader
(Plato's philosopher king) is one
strategy. The wise leader says what
to do and everyone does it. While
this has, on occasion, worked for
decades at a time, leaders are subject to change without notice (by
dying, being overthrown, suffering breakdowns of various
sorts, or losing their perspective or integrity in the giddy
heights of power). So philosopher kings present a problem:
they change, and not always appropriately for the society.
Maybe it would help to depend on more than one person.

We now have the capacity for communities and societies to be their own wise philosopher kings.

The idea behind the Soviet Communist Party was that it,
as a collective entity, would be the wise leader, the vanguard
of the proletariat. Its Central Committee would come up with
what to do, then everyone would do it. The main weakness of
this approach proved to be Lord Acton's infamous saying: "All
power tends to corrupt. Absolute power corrupts absolutely."
Once the Party and its individual members based their calcu-
lations on their own—rather than the society's—best interests,
the "vanguard approach" became very questionable as a strat-

egy for social intelligence. Also, as Soviet society grew more complex, it became harder to manage from a central point.

Which brings us to democracy. The basic principle of democracy is that those affected by a decision will make it. This inherently decentrist, creative, responsive strategy is a leap forward that has one main problem: It assumes that people are able and willing to make intelligent decisions in groups.

Since this is not always the case, we've evolved what we call "representative democracy" where we choose philosopher kings (e.g., presidents) and vanguard committees (e.g., Congresses) to make our decisions for us, throwing them out when we don't like what they do. This has a rough sort of workability. In election years everyone takes a bit of time to review the society's problems and possible solutions and, at least in theory, chooses the best solutions and wisest persons to empower for the next few years.

Unfortunately, this strategy is also undone by Lord Acton's prophecy. Representation centralizes power, and that centralized power attracts corrupting influences to itself (especially from other centralized powers in the society like corporations). So we balance it with all sorts of interest groups, grassroots movements, unions, legal checks and balances, etc. American history is a beautiful tale of democracy progressing and regressing at the same time in the most remarkable ways, evolving as it goes. Unfortunately we can't afford too many more democratic regressions (concentrations of power): our social problems are so great, change is happening so fast and human power is growing so rapidly that we are confronted with a daunting choice: make our next quantum leap in societal intelligence or collapse as a culture.

Our challenge is, simply, to learn how to become not only democratic but wisely democratic as individuals, as groups and as a society. We need to

- learn how to generate a spirit of partnership (non-domination) among ourselves—and create resilient institutions that embed the practice of partnership in our culture and impede the familiar corruptions of power;
- increase our individual responsibility and co-leadership abilities—and create institutions that empower emergent, self-organizing, situational, and collaborative leadership;
- master consensual group dynamics and communication skills—and create institutions that practice, facilitate and promote high quality communication;
- creatively utilize our diversity (including our differences of opinion and style)—and create institutions that welcome and productively facilitate diverse people, ideas, and styles to develop themselves with clarity and to serve the common good;
- increase the accessibility of information and other resources—and create institutions that ensure society has what it needs to function well and evolve wisely; and

- nurture our own and one another's deep realization of our needs, our stories, our values and our capabilities—and create institutions that support us in that and in working together in all our rich uniqueness.

There are many ways to do each of these, and there are probably other things we need to do, as well.

This is a new field of investigation and activism. We need to clarify what is required—and how to do it—to enable our societal intelligence. Then we need to spread these understandings and practices into the society. To the extent we succeed, I suspect our groups and our society will start behaving intelligently, quite naturally.

But there's a significance to all this that goes beyond democracy and saving our hides from extinction. To the extent we achieve societal intelligence, it seems to me that we will shift to a different kind of society entirely. The evolutionary leap may be equivalent to the evolution of individual intelligence. We may reach a state in which societies become intelligent entities—neither a monolith unified by conformity nor a machine made of fragmented individuals, but a thinking organism made of discrete participants, each contributing their unique and essential creativity into the dynamic wisdom and power of the whole.

Or maybe not. Maybe it will just be a good society to live in. Either way, it seems to me worth working for.

Ultimately, Global Catastrophe is About Life

...and life is about
what is possible for Life,
to which the answer is
always itself
over and over.
So let us party for possibility
and fill the streets with our passion,
going straight for the hearts
of a culture that is about to learn
to live again.

Yes: real joy needs to be freed,
but not because its face is smiling.
Real joy needs to be freed,
because the Sun pulls buds into being.
The real tears need to be sobbed.
Not because they are tears,
but because they are real.
The real gifts have to be given,
not because they will make someone happy,
but because giving is the river of life
along which all things become possible.

So it is time to leave the stale anxieties
of dead-end cultures
and join the belly laugh and cry of possibility

on behalf of Life
and dance the night away
with our tears
because they are real.

For the night is with us always,
above even the bluest sky,
yet it is criss-crossed with light
from as far away as the beginning of time,
booming and radiant.

And we will find that our dancing with catastrophe
(even our running away from it)
takes us into the
hungry, unemployed, disabled, extinct
parts of ourselves
where we get to choose
to fall apart
or become more whole
or both.

Life is only asking us
to bring our full selves
to the party
every moment,
with our souls planted solidly
in laughter, dinner, one another and the Earth.
And if we leave behind

our tears, our pain, our confusion
and our urge to touch one another
the party is dead,
the party is of the dead.
Not that death doesn't belong at the party;
It does.
Death knows the difference
between what is real and what is not.

It is all real.
It is all coming home together.
The end and the beginning
are waking up in the same mist.
This is our chance.

| ✳ |

Reflections on

Systems

Chapter Twenty

Caring and systemic awareness: Does compassion itself need to evolve?

Everyone and everything on Earth is now more intimately connected to everyone and everything else than ever before—through global culture and telecommunications, trade and finance, pollution and climate, wars, terrorism and other social disturbances, technological developments and species extinctions, and the growing hopes and fears about our shared future.

This overarching reality has created one of the most disturbing spiritual paradoxes of our era:

Caring for one part of the whole can be detrimental to other parts of the whole in ways we may not even realize.

So we find ourselves pressed and called to expand our circles of caring, our feelings of love, the nature of our compassion. Our old forms of concern and fellow-feeling are becoming not only inadequate, but may even in some circumstances be counter-productive.

With industrial-strength health care and agriculture, we support exploding populations and deteriorating topsoil, aquifers, and forests. We address poverty with efforts to increase the affluence of the poor, further stressing Earth's support systems. With a flight to an environmental conference, we add a year's worth of CO_2 to our carbon footprint, just from the jet emissions. We fund charities and good causes, but not activities designed to change the systems that continually generate the problems our philanthropy targets.

We need more systemic consciousness. We need a compassion and caring that looks beyond the immediate suffering, destruction, and death of individuals, groups, animals, and natural places to address long-term consequences and, in particular, the underlying causes and systemic dynamics that give rise to our perennial struggles and emerging crises. We need systemic awareness embedded in a larger evolutionary awareness about how things unfold and why.

Systemic awareness would suggest that if we are going to reduce deaths, we need to reduce births, or else the system will be thrown out of balance. Systemic awareness suggests that we should do more virtual and local conferencing to reduce climate impacts. Systemic awareness suggests we should develop agricultural practices and technologies that preserve and renew precious resources like aquifers, topsoil, and forests. Systemic awareness suggests not only that consumerism and material economic growth are unsustainable but that life is better served by finding rewards in non-material prosperity—in spiritual abundance, rich relationships, vibrant community, lush nature, rewarding creativity, deep meaning, and the many simple pleasures of life uncluttered with "stuff".

We don't have to ship toxic products 12,000 miles to create good lives for all the world's people. We don't have to have everyone spend a lot of money to have a healthy economy. We don't have to keep individuals alive against their wills at tremendous expense in order to value human life.

If we want to defend the rights and sanctity of individual human life, we need to come to terms with the fact that certain protections and benefits for one individual (or type of individual) may well harm or prevent help to other individuals (or types of individuals). Ultimately, honest concern for all individuals requires that we address social problems from systemic perspectives, where they impact everyone.

We need to address the sources of pollution, war, poverty, and all the other causes of suffering, death and destruction. We need to deal with our money- and profit-centered economic systems; our adversarial, manipulated political and governance systems; our cultural stories about how separate we are from nature and one another; the dynamics that leave us "with no time" yet engage us in endless distractions from what urgently needs attention; the resource-intensive technologies and land-use policies that make it so hard for individuals to be environmentally responsible; and more.

If we don't think systemically, our caring ends up favoring the rights and value of some lives over the rights and value of others. Not only do we neglect the activities that could make a real difference in the long run, but our caring becomes less and less effective, because of our interconnectedness. In our efforts to provide health care to all citizens we deny health care to the illegal immigrants who care for our children and crops and who, when sick with a contagious illness, spread it to the citizens we were trying to care for in the first place.

Evolutionary compassion stretches us from only caring for parts to caring for the whole

Such short-sighted, skewed, ultimately counter-productive caring is, of course, easy to promote in a system that encourages advocacy of narrow self-interest over the common good, and shallow partisan agendas over deep deliberation that would reveal vital interconnections and complex causes. Politics becomes a battleground rather than a collaborative effort to wisely meet universal human needs, pursue shared aspirations, and care for the natural world that supports us all.

Energy expended in such battles does little to benefit the vast majority, and divides natural allies to the benefit of special interests manipulating the public conversation. Redesigning our political system to tap into our natural collaborative tendencies (rather than our natural competitive tendencies) would do wonders for a resurgence of effective caring. Experience shows that groups of ordinary people convened and assisted to find good solutions on behalf of their community don't sit around fighting with one another. They rise to the occasion, transcend or creatively use their differences, and usually come up with proposals that make more sense to more people than the lopsided compromises that emerge from the business as usual partisan battles.

Being a responsible part of the system

As we become more systemically aware, we see that the meaning of morality, ethics and caring are changing radically as our ability increases to impact people and natural systems miles away or years in the future, often in ways that are hard to see in time to effectively change our behavior. This shift undermines the reliability of simple, direct person-to-person caring and decent behavior. Nowadays, even as we caringly act, we can do great harm.

To me, this suggests a four-part ethic to guide our caring within a systemic context:

1. **Keep caring.** Understand that in a technological age our natural compassion—though no longer enough—is still vital. Stay grounded in caring. Help one another. Develop compassion for and communion with our neighbors. And then...

2.   Stretch into systemic awareness. Expand and deepen our awareness and caring in space, time, and subtlety. Learn to think systemically (considering interconnections and "side effects") and holistically (considering the whole, the big picture, the long term, multi-level phenomena) within the evolutionary perspective (considering our place in the vast story of emergent complexity). Understand more about the larger dynamics in which—and through which—we operate. Learn to sense systems—natural, economic, social—operating through us in our everyday lives. Assume interdependence. Be cautious and humble in the face of the unknown, which is always much, much larger than what we know. Stretch our instinctual caring for the immediate, obvious welfare of ourselves and those we easily love, into caring for those affected by our socio-economic system, for life forms that are unlike us, for the health of ecosystemic dynamics (like climate, chemical cycles, predator-prey relationships) that are hard to see, and for effects that are distant in space and time (especially for impacts on "the seventh generation after us").

3.   Develop local systems. Reduce the range of our impact. Become indigenous, local. Try to localize as much economic, political, and other activity as possible into communities and bioregions. Help the flow of materials be small, local and cyclical. Build conscious, obviously interdependent relationships. In local systems, we can better trust our natural caring impulses (to care for what is immediately around us) because the effects of our actions are primarily local. Since local answerability "feedback loops" are more immediate, any needed corrections can be more readily accomplished locally.

4. Build powerful feedback into nonlocal systems to educate and channel our caring. We need help to experience the consequences of our individual and collective behaviors when those impacts are far away in space or time. Sometimes this help comes in the form of information (like statistics or pictures), sometimes in the form of direct stimulus to behave in certain ways (like prices or blackouts). This empowers the stretch of system awareness in #2, above, using education and discipline and an informed use of technology and the arts to compensate for the natural limitations of our five senses: Individually we may not be built to comprehend "the big picture"; but collectively, we have the capacity and imperative to do so.

Effective caring demands that we experience systems, either locally or through media and education

This four-part ethic expands and clarifies the environmentalist slogan *Think globally, act locally.* The slogan works well to the extent our global thoughts and local actions are informed by multi-level understandings, co-creative culture and systemic feedback. This won't happen on its own. It requires intentional action.

There are (and could be more) videos, art, stories, plays, field trips, etc., designed to help our limited senses *see* the effects of our individual and collective actions and the dynamics through which we participate in creating those effects.

There are (and could be more) guided meditations to expand our hearts, to sensitize us, and to make us mindful of the less-visible lives and living communities with whom we share this world.

There are (and could be more) statistics collected—including participatory "crowd-sourced" data gathering—to give us better feedback about the effects we are creating, and about our shared circumstances, from which we could then caringly and effectively act.

There is (and could be more) legislation to protect the health of our shared natural and human communities and future generations, as well as (and even sometimes instead of) individual and corporate rights and welfare.

A personal challenge for all of us

Expanding our heart-based compassion and caring to embrace system-based compassion and caring is not easy.

It is hard for me to turn away from suffering individuals— from homeless people on the street, from tsunami victims in Southeast Asia, from my own partner with cancer—in order to focus on efforts to transform the economic and political systems that make such suffering common. Each time I focus on one, I am painfully aware of the calling of the other.

It is hard for me to turn away from environmental devastation—from the clear-cut a few miles from my home, from the polar bears who will soon have no ice and seals to hunt, from the toxic island of plastic garbage in the mid-Pacific, twice as large as Texas—in order to focus on efforts to shift the culture and social systems that make such destruction inevitable. Again, each time I focus on one—the causes *or* the effects—I am painfully aware of the calling of the other.

This shift from palpable realities to the seemingly abstract "systems"—and the effort to hold both at once in our consciousness—is hard on our minds and even harder on our hearts. Sometimes I wonder if the challenge we experience here is the sensation of stretching demanded of us as we evolve into a more whole form of humanity in which heart-based compassion and system-based compassion merge into one higher form of insight and engagement.

But we aren't there yet. And at our current stage of development, I want to challenge us all to honestly ask—over and over—whether traditional "love," "caring," and "compassion" are themselves adequate to motivate and guide our life-affirming work in the twenty-first century. I think we need to reframe what we mean by love, caring and compassion for this new era, to include a bigger web of causation, experience, and transformative possibility.

For without understanding factors such as those discussed in this chapter, love, caring and compassion are more likely to provide only artificial legs for the children who step in land mines, shelters for the battered women, advertisements

Social systems shape everyday actions to enhance or degrade life, and make caring easy or hard

for the blue whale, charity for those displaced by violent storms, seed banks for extinct species.

If we act only out of our deep loving kindness, global economics and its addictive culture and corrosive politics and media could well continue to move deeper into the heart of all Life, starving, alienating, and blowing up more children, eroding more relationships and communities, destroying the habitats of more animals slipping away forever into extinction, killing vast oceans which were the Source of Life, and destabilizing the global climate which was the womb of our civilization so many millennia ago.

We have an opportunity to grow into a civilization that has no need for land mines, where few go hungry, a world that has few battered women or species driven to extinction, where the storms that rage are those that renew the Earth without wreaking havoc on human communities, and where oceans and forests swarm with abundance once again.

To take that opportunity, not only do our minds and hearts need to grow into systemic and evolutionary awareness, but our social systems themselves need to embody such awareness and provide us with the guidance we need to care deeply and effectively and to take action to bring the fruits of that renewed caring to the world.

The new sensibility and systems we are being called to develop will, if we develop them, raise human civilization to a far higher level than it has ever achieved before. I like to imagine us becoming *Homo sapiens holisticus*—humans who are wise on behalf of the whole, whose compassion encompasses the world.

So how can our hearts mature into this bigger sensibility of service, which seems so abstract and yet is so urgently needed?

Transformational economist Robert Theobald once suggested that the worst thing about modern society was the way things were set up made it so hard to effectively care. Perhaps we can develop sufficient educated, holistic[14], systemically sophisticated caring among us to generate the kind of culture and social systems in which simple caring once again naturally produces good outcomes.

It would be such a great relief—and very healthy for the Earth and all of us.

---

[14] See footnote 5, page 147.

What We Long For

Gravity is just another name
for the deep longing of every part of the universe
for every other part.

The longing that wells up in the universe
is the longing that brings forth
everything that is next,
that is now,
that is tomorrow,
that ever was.

We were born of that longing.
We ARE that longing.

And what we long for,
  who we want to be with,
  what we want to become,
  what we want to see in the world—
and how we respond to these longings—
is our calling,
  is the upwelling of Earth's longing
   for the promise of what's next
    for the unfolding possibility
     that we call evolution.

❘ ✳ ❘

Chapter Twenty-One

What makes a social system conscious?

In May 2005 at the first Evolutionary Salon, thirty scientists, evolutionary theologians and social activists envisioned

an emerging movement
for the conscious evolution
of increasingly conscious social systems.

That's an intriguing idea. But what does it mean? What *is* a conscious social system?

It turns out that this is a rich inquiry, juicy and productive, moving us more broadly and deeply into life, as any evolutionary inquiry should. What do we find on that journey?

One way for a social system to be conscious is for more of us who are in it to be informed about—and oriented to—the social system's life and wellbeing. Our many individual consciousnesses can then add up to a form of collective consciousness. Sometimes a collective "field of consciousness" permeates the whole system.

Consider a mundane example: Think about what happens when millions of us—all at the same time—watch a catastrophe like a tsunami, a disastrous hurricane, or a couple of giant skyscrapers collapsing, on television news and the Internet. Together, as we watch and react, we generate a palpable field of awareness and concern that powerfully shapes subsequent events. Similar to the way magnetic and gravitational fields work, in this field of shared awareness every person and institution shifts in relationship to it.

Perhaps the most important shared awareness that we have is our collective identity—a shared perception that we *are* our group, community, country, or world. This recognition underlies most other aspects of collective consciousness. The more deeply we sense our common identity and the more care and esteem we have for one another and for the larger life we are part of, the more the human systems we live in emerge as coherent—and potentially conscious—entities. In well-developed forms of collective identity, we not only cherish our whole community, bioregion, or world, but see it living in and through us—cherishing every part of itself, every individual or species, as a source of diverse delight and unique gifts. In this expansive form of identity we can often experience a deep, flowing communion.

So what is possible when we become a coherent living system together? To the extent more of us know what's going on ... *and* care about what's happening to our whole community, society, and world ... *and* are linked to one another in useful ways ... *and* know what to do to improve our system's wellbeing ... our system, as a whole, will become more conscious. As these factors grow, we *collectively* tend to act more and more like a coherent living organism that appropriately responds to the world around it. Our community, society or world shows up as a living conscious whole.

A social system's consciousness includes and transcends our own

So the consciousness of a whole social system naturally includes our individual consciousnesses. But more is involved. How are our individual minds informed, linked, attuned, engaged...? To answer this, we need to explore the structures, processes, and cultures that are as much "the system" as we are.

What makes a social *system* conscious?

Understanding more about the factors that constitute whole-system consciousness can help us clarify where to focus our attention, resources and efforts to advance the healthy evolution of humanity.

Here are four qualities of a conscious social system:

- *Holistic/Multi-level awareness*
- *Shared knowledge and care*
- *Systemic self-leadership*
- *Evolvability*

In exploring each one of these below, I begin with a defining inquiry, followed by a description of what we might experience in an idealized conscious social system.

Holistic/Multi-level awareness

How do we deeply and consciously connect to the whole systems we are part of, including all the levels that are part of it?

To the extent we live in a conscious social system, more of us know, identify with, and care about our group, community, bioregion, and world—each system we are part of—as an entity itself—a whole. We are very aware of the existence and needs of these precious living systems, through culture (especially stories), education, governance, and spiritual and group attunement practices.

We know about the health of our human and natural communities, thanks to engaging media stories, grassroots sharing of news, quality of life statistics, briefings, clear attention to environmental changes and many other common activities and facets of our culture. We know enough about system dynamics to recognize what is happening, what it means, and how we can engage with it.

Our system itself is rich with collective forms of perception—from satellite sensors, to statistics and the visualization tools that display them (such as Chris Jordan's art), to telescopes and microscopes and macroscopes (computers and other resources that look into complexity the way telescopes look into space), to journalists and observant, articulate citizens who share their distributed seeing and hearing (from crowdsourcing to shared videos).

We are aware of and value one another, and what people different from us—who are part of the same system—are doing. The field of our collective awareness is vitally alive, evidenced by how often similar ideas, innovations, and discoveries show up simultaneously in different places, as needed.

Shared knowledge and care

How do human knowing and caring flow powerfully through the social system?

To the extent we live in a conscious social system, the relevant knowledge or caring of one person, time or place is, to a remarkable degree, available to other people, times and places. Throughout our healthy media, communication, research, education, government and political systems, new knowledge and forms of caring are born and information and care flow freely, intermingling in many ways and increasing in value as they move.

Our whole systems have forms of memory which transcend our individual memories and lives. These include traditional forms such as culture and stories, as well as more recent forms like powerfully inclusive and accessible information storage, evaluation, distribution, and retrieval systems like libraries, databases, open source intelligence services, and the searchable Internet.

We readily find one another to work together and share what we care about, and systemic structures and processes facilitate this—from electronic networking tools to self-organizing face-to-face gatherings around advertised interests (such as Open Space conferences).

The flow and exchange of life energy and awareness through the system helps it respond to changing conditions

Systemic self-leadership

How are behavior, power and social guidance systems aligned to serve the needs of the whole?

To the extent we live in a conscious social system, our political, economic and social arrangements ensure that our self-interested behaviors naturally contribute to the welfare of the whole—and that we collectively empower our leaders and institutions to serve the whole.

Our social arrangements make it difficult for any of us—especially our leaders and power centers—to unduly colonize our systems' resources for personal or sub-group benefit at the expense of the whole. Well-designed future-orientation systems and feedback mechanisms—including learning systems, norms, contests, rewards and punishments, and more—keep us responsive to the needs of our whole community, society, and world. (This relates to systemic consciousness because when social power centers parasitize a social system for their own benefit, they tend to distort that system's knowledge, awareness, and caring sub-systems to the detriment of the whole.)

To the extent we live in a conscious social system, our political, governmental, economic, information and education systems are designed for answerability and service to the common good—while mindfully protecting and nurturing our rich individuality and diversity from which so many social benefits flow. Powerful feedback loops and collective learning and oversight systems prevent irresponsible power from growing cancerously or corrupting our beloved culture of self-organization and wise participatory leadership.

Our institutions and cultural practices support legitimate leadership arising from the collective intelligence and wisdom generated by adequately diverse groups of us in high quality conversations, which are watched by our whole community or society and often exercise direct decision-making power (such as informed, ad hoc citizen deliberative councils).

Evolvability

How does a whole system evolve itself?

To the extent our system is conscious, it constantly reflects (sometimes through its leaders, representatives or proxies, as above) on its own operation, the results of our collective activity, and our future prospects—making changes as needed.

Key parts of our systems are kept as free as possible from bias, fixed ideas, and inflexible attitudes. We honor wholeness in all its forms at every level. Our system continually and creatively engages the diversity—and even strangeness, extremism, and conflict—in and around it to generate inclusive, evolving forms of common sense and shared enterprise. Many ways to do this are broadly known and used.

We have a certain eagerness to welcome, generate and consider novel perspectives and possibilities—and to test them in useful ways. Our mainstream honors and maintains a productive relationship with our fringes.

We set up our systemic structures so they can and do change in a timely manner: They neither resist needed changes and miss promising opportunities nor do they change chaotically in response to every impulse. Overall, we maintain a healthy relationship between centralized and decentralized forms of collective perception, reflection, and action (such as subsidiarity)—out of which the right level of appropriate change naturally emerges.

A movement for the evolution of increasingly conscious social systems is already emerging. Tens of thousands of people are developing ways that increase people's holistic, multi-level, multi-modal, systemic awareness. Systems for sharing knowledge and effective caring are cropping up all over, along with breakthrough methods for corporate, community, and network self-organization. All around us systems in crisis are rapidly evolving and every week brings new ways to do this evolution more consciously.

Evolutionary activists can encourage those already involved in this movement to become more aware of the evolutionary significance of what they are doing. They can add to its power, effectiveness and meaning by framing it in deep-time evolutionary terms and by advocating and facilitating the creation of new institutions and cultures that make these collective capacities permanent, natural parts of our humanity.

Note: *Some researchers suggest developmental sequences in the evolution of awareness—for example, from*
- *reactivity (automatic responsiveness to environmental stimuli) to*
- *awareness (subjective experience, especially of a coherent or mapped "reality", including dream states) to*
- *consciousness (awake orientation to what's actually in and around oneself) to*
- *self-awareness or reflexive consciousness (consciousness of one's own consciousness and its dynamics) to*
- *transcendent or transpersonal awareness (merging with a consciousness that includes and transcends one's own).*

This has intriguing implications for the consciousness of social systems, e.g., designing for automatic systemic health and responsiveness (reactivity) or for mass awareness of and intentional engagement with the dynamics of collective intelligence (reflexive consciousness). I see these as useful distinctions calling for more in-depth, nuanced exploration and application to social systems.

You can't hide anymore

I saw you
in the water
making hydrogen
out of cosmic plasmoid shrapnel
making oxygen
out of star-bellies burning.

I saw you hiding in the rains and floods
flowing camouflaged from faucets
as if you were only liquid
as if you could get inside me
without being spotted
as the Creator

as if you could hide
in the conversations of the world
in the sweat and tears of love and pain
in the green exchange of trees and Pan
in each back room and digital screen
in the flow of my own caring creativity
you blessing the world, being the world,
unseen.

| ✳ |

Reflections on

an

Evolutionary Activism
Movement

Chapter Twenty-Two

A rationale and guide for nonviolence as a basis for conscious evolutionary activism

I offer this essay as an example of how we can explore a particular political or activist approach from an evolutionary perspective. In this case, the topic is nonviolence, a compelling option in a multi-centric global civilization rife with conflict, where weapons of mass destruction are being developed, spreading, and always susceptible to both deliberate and accidental use.

However, there is another, perhaps more important reason for the inclusion of this essay. Previous studies have provided evolutionary rationales for domination, war, and violence. In a healthy evolutionary activist movement, diverse political and activist approaches —including archetypal political ideologies like liberalism, conservatism, communism, and libertarianism —would all be advocated and critiqued from an evolutionary perspective. Evolutionary science and philosophy would provide a common foundation for in-depth inquiry, scholarship and debate.

The views presented in this book—including its focus on conversation, green economics, and nonviolence—arise from my own experience and beliefs. However, one of my hopes is that this book will demonstrate in a more general way the value of using the evolutionary perspective as a lens through which to view our current situation and all the various approaches to dealing with it. Through thoughtful conversations among widely diverse advocates and critics, the evolutionary activist ecosystem would evolve more inclusive, potent forms of evolutionary activism.

*As far as this essay is concerned, readers will find extensive guidance here, in some detail, based on a single organizing principle. All the guidelines offered here interpenetrate one another. Due to the density of this material, some readers may prefer to skim or browse to "get the gist" or check for specific points of interest or simply move on to Chapters 23-25, which envision what an evolutionary activist **movement** would be like.*

The overarching evolutionary guidance for activists using nonviolence as the basis for their work on social systems is this:

> **In any situation or system, seek ways to replace force with consciousness.**

Force, in this context, refers to the use of coercion or overwhelming strength or power to dominate, control, or otherwise get one's way, often against resistance. The power used can be physical, economic, social, intellectual, emotional, military, psychological, technological, etc. The more force used, the less we take into account the nature or needs of the Other. The more we take the Other into account, the less force and resources we need to accomplish mutual ends.

Consciousness, the capacity to be aware, in this context, includes all the interior dimensions and capacities of life that can—among other things—help us deal successfully with our changing world by sensing, understanding and creatively, collaboratively relating to the conditions in us and the entities, interactions, and contexts around us.

This evolutionary moment challenges us to bring the power of consciousness to bear on the process of self-reflective evolution itself to replace the creative violence of supernovas, life-and-death struggles, and wars with highly aware intelligence, wisdom, and care.

So as evolutionary activists, we seek to replace force everywhere,

- in every **entity** (every individual, group and system);

- in every **interaction** (every conversation, exchange, conflict, and engagement with nature);

- in every **context** (every situation, culture, gathering, community and urban design); and

- in every form of consciousness (in all sensing, learning, visioning, morality, and all other forms of thinking, feeling and experience).

Note that many of our technologies, tools, cultures, infrastructures, and systems are extensions or manifestations of our consciousness at collective levels. They reflect what we, as a people, think and feel. From highways and militaries to social services and financial systems, they proclaim our alienation, our communion, our fear, our greed, our respect, our understanding, and our ignorance. This reality is of particular interest to evolutionary agents seeking to transform social systems. It helps us understand the larger stories we are co-creating and living and where they need to shift.

There is, of course, an evolutionary logic to this mandate to replace force with consciousness. The more we expand our awareness, understanding, care, intelligence, imagination and other forms of consciousness—especially wisdom— the less we need—or want—to force things. This principle underlies our development of levers, negotiation, democracy, permaculture and numerous other innovations with which we have built civilization. We learn how to work *with* the entities and circumstances we've come to understand, instead of just forcing them to do our will, thus saving ourselves a lot of energy. Efficient use of energy is a major selective factor in evolution. (Kreuzer, 2007)

This evolutionary dynamic unfolds in a developmental progression. It starts when we learn—from experience, science, or technology—how to control and manipulate the physical world and life more efficiently, elegantly, and effectively to get what we want through understanding the "laws" or patterns of nature, of engineering, of psychology, etc. With our understanding of thermodynamics, we create engines. With our under- *To the extent we* standing of the psychology of target *understand* markets we influence citizens to vote *something, we* for our candidate or buy our product. This is the manipulation stage, one *know how to* step above brute force. *creatively*

Our consciousness then evolves *engage it* towards true collaboration, where we— *without force* you and I, us and our adversaries, humankind and nature—help each other get what we each need and want—in cooperatives, family conversations, in deliberative democracy, in Nonviolent Communication, in permaculture.

Now the role of consciousness further evolves into increasing recognition of our essential communion, within which our differences can be used creatively, generating greater wholeness. Here our consciousness serves the co-creation of previously unimagined shared enterprises and civilizations. Emerging examples include the Earth Charter, or the global grassroots upsurge of catastrophe relief after hurricanes and tsunamis.

As evolutionary activists we seek to use these last two forms of consciousness, especially, and to make them central characteristics of the emerging global culture. Social processes and institutions that embody these forms of consciousness help social systems themselves become conscious.

This shift from force to consciousness is the fulcrum of human evolution at this critical time—at individual, collective, and systemic scales.

As we reach our planetary limits, the downsides of force, violence, and control become increasingly obvious. Our technological and social capacities to generate harm through our efforts to force, impact, and control people and life—no matter how well intended—threaten our extinction.

Step by step, in more and more areas of life, we are discovering that the use of force—and, in fact, the use of any imposed energy—is intimately tied to our failure to adequately understand the whole picture of what we are dealing with. This is perhaps most poignantly the case when we ignore or misconstrue the lessons coming to us in the form of persistent or increasing disturbances—dissent, illnesses, wars, problems, environmental degradation, and so on. Instead of learning from them as signs of something deeper to attend to, we try to deny them or solve them at a superficial level so we can persist doing the things that created the trouble in the first place. We go further out on a limb that can't continue to support us. Paying deep attention earlier in the process will help us develop the kinds of understanding we need to fully deal with issues in ways that do not demand repeated or continual attention.

The more fully we understand, the less force or energy we need or want to use. The less energy we use to serve any given need, the more efficient and elegant our systems and behaviors become, making them favored by natural selection and the general directionality of evolution. Furthermore, the height of efficiency is elegance, which tends, as well, to be inspiring, enjoyable, attractive, and/or beautiful, in its own right, thereby engaging people in spreading and sustaining it.

This guidance serves at every level—individual and collective. Given our focus here on transforming social systems, we are concentrating on its application to social systems. Below are explorations of how this guidance applies to evolutionary *means*—the ways we do our evolutionary activist work—and how it applies to evolutionary *action*—the things we are actually working on through our evolutionary activism.

Guidance concerning evolutionary means

Force is the option we use when we don't talk and listen to one another, when we can't handle diversity, when we can't deal with dissonance, and when we don't want to include what repels us in our biased, oversimplified views about life.

Evolutionary activists aim to move beyond those dynamics, as much as possible. The guidelines in A-D below explore how evolutionary agents can *live* the guidance about replacing force with consciousness in their evolutionary work.

- **A** addresses the role of *conversation*.
- **B** talks about creative use of *diversity*.
- **C** explores how to handle *dissonance*.
- **D** discusses deep, *inclusive simplicity*.

A. Support a culture of dialogue, deliberation, and all other forms of generative conversation. Generative conversation is the means through which we

Evolutionary activists use dialogue to help diverse people move through dissonance to inclusive simplicity

expand and apply our consciousness together. It is the primary medium of human co-creative interaction from which needed evolutionary change can emerge, especially when we wish to minimize force, violence, and control. Our sustained collective conscious evolution will be possible to the extent we develop, use, and spread the art and culture of generative conversation. (Atlee, 2003; Holman et al, 2007)

B. Creatively engage diversity and uniqueness to support greater wholeness. Evolution happens through the iterative interaction of diverse entities. Diversity is always part of every problem and every solution, for it is part of every whole. The uniqueness of people and circumstances, adequately appreciated, is an almost endless resource. Diversity is vital for resilience, covering all bases in times of uncertainty. Every unique individual, idea, passion, solution, perspective, mode of knowing—each one has gifts and limitations and is part of some big picture we need to understand. Paradoxically, heartfelt expression of difference—if well heard—can connect unique individuals into a lived experience of the whole, replacing cultural tendencies towards conformity, isolation, and groupthink. When disturbance appears, it is the cry of a voice that has not yet found its place in the whole. It prompts asking who else or what else should be included here? Help bring them—with all their differences and conflicts—into a bigger picture, a broader solution which includes and transcends their unique gifts and limitations. We can only do this by including diverse people, perspectives, and information at every step of the way. To be truly inclusive and to tap into larger realities, we also need to include and integrate diverse forms of intelligence and expression—linear and nonlinear, analytic and aesthetic, head, heart and body (Gardner, 1983).

C. **Engage creatively with dissonance**—disturbance, problems, conflicts, crises, suffering, even passions and dreams. These are all opportunities for breakthrough. Evolution happens most readily in challenging, dissonant contexts where business as usual is being shaken up. Using this guidance involves designing and stimulating iterative creative interactions—especially conversations guided by powerful questions—which welcome and catalyze dissonant energies into evolutionary leaps. Paradoxically, this includes creating "safe environments" in which people can engage challenges more consciously. So we need to develop our capacity to welcome and facilitate this dance of safety and challenge. (See Action guidance 2 below.)

D. **Seek the elegant, inclusive simplicity** on the other side of messy complexity. Ideology, arrogance, and narrow-mindedness achieve their simplicity by rejecting whole realms of reality or understanding. This narrowing of consciousness often triggers the use of force to control the realms we do not understand. In contrast, the kind of simplicity that human evolution now requires is that which integrates many differ-

Health *means* *relationships* *among the* *parts support* *the continuing* *functionality* *of the whole*

ent entities and factors into useful solutions and worldviews that have recognizable integrity. More often than not, the path to such elegant wholeness takes us through the messiness of all the relevant factors that don't seem to fit together at first. Our task—which calls us to greater courage, curiosity, and humility—is to seek, through open inquiry, the more inclusive insights available at

the unpredictable end of that journey. This demands a courageous pioneering spirit. But once accomplished, "the simplicity on the other side of complexity" usually leaps out as an elegant awakening—an ah-ha! or a wow!—where what was previously messy and fragmented resolves into a more powerful, appealing, and wholesome picture of who we are and what is possible. In the process, we often move beyond otherness: People, systems, and situations we saw (and often neglected or rejected) as unrelated to us suddenly become part of a larger whole that includes us and engages our life energy. Erstwhile enemies and strangers become part of humanity. Climate change becomes a matter of our children's survival and relates to our behavior today. Suddenly we find ourselves embedded in realities with which we had no relation before, and they become part of us. We awaken to our intimate kinship with the Other, our embodiment of the systems we live in, and an expansion of our sense of self to embrace what was once background context.

Guidance concerning realms of evolutionary action

To the extent human systems try to survive and succeed by using force and self-interested manipulation, they will perish. The energy they need to function, the feedback they ignore, the impossibility of controlling increasingly complex systems, and the resistance they encounter will all undermine their success.

The guidance below embraces the kinds of change through which evolutionary agents seek to call forth healthier and more conscious human systems, while making force increasingly unnecessary and unattractive.

- 1 deals with the health of the systems themselves.
- 2 deals with contexts and systemic awareness of them.
- 3 deals with the systemic capacity to effectively respond to complex, changing circumstances.

Evolutionary action to catalyze systemic evolution notably follows the following guidelines, each of which includes several examples of its application.

1. Cultivate healthy self-organization. Create conditions in which the system's complex interactions cohere in ways that sustain its health with minimal investment of energy and attention. (Alexander, 1977; Ecotrust, 2000) Among the actions that contribute to healthy self-organization are:

- *Cultivate healthy behavior:* Evolution generates new sustainable entities to the extent their constituent entities behave in ways that serve the wellbeing of the larger whole they are part of. Therefore, evolutionary activists set up systems in which individuals, corporations, and countries readily act in ways that promote the well being of whole communities, societies, and ecosystems. This may include laws and incentives that restrain unwanted behaviors; full cost accounting in our economic systems; education and epiphanies through which people experience their place in the Larger Aliveness within and around them.

- *Cultivate healthy power:* The evolution and sustainability of social systems requires cooperation among empowered constituents. Therefore, evolutionary activists nurture a culture of power-with (cooperation and synergy) and power-from-within (authenticity and integrity). Wherever power-over (domination and control) seems needed, evolutionary activists make sure it is balanced, distributed and/or answerable to those over whom it is exercised.[15] This prevents para-

---

[15] See "Democracy: A social power analysis" by John Atlee
co-intelligence.org/CIPol_democSocPwrAnal.html

sitic accumulations of power that degrade the whole to benefit a powerful part. This may include collaborative group process; meditation; mediation; campaign finance reform and constraints on corporate power; and collaborative approaches to nature like permaculture (Mollison, 1990) and biomimicry (Benyus, 2002).

- *Cultivate healthy flow:* Evolution favors efficiency in the use of energy, materials, and information. The more readily these can flow in a complex system, the better constituent entities and systems can coordinate. Therefore evolutionary activists support the open, elegant flow of energy, materials, and information to wherever it best serves the wellbeing and evolvability of the system and the people and groups in it. This may include freedom of the Internet and media; sunshine and privacy laws; recycling and emission controls; green local economics (Henderson 1991; Hawken et al, 2000; Korten, 2006); systems of mutual benefit; and more evolutionary forms of philanthropy.

2. Cultivate healthy systemic contexts that both nurture and challenge people in them. Evolution involves diverse entities interacting in contexts that shape, test, and nurture them. Context is an active participant in whatever happens. Context is as important as who we are and what we do, because *it powerfully shapes* who we are and what we do. It behooves us to be aware of the contexts around us and the roles they play in what's happening. Together, we can consciously shape the systems, stories, and other contexts that shape us. We need to remember that contexts can be nurturing and/or challenging—in ways that serve or undermine life. With this in mind, we want to be more conscious of them so we can support those that nurture and challenge us to promote the wellbeing of current and future generations, and to create societies where such contexts are the norm. Here are some areas for our work with contexts:

- *Healthy social context.* Become more aware of social conditions and nurture relationships, norms, institutions and social situations that both support and challenge the people in them to enhance the wellbeing of current and future generations.

- *Healthy contexts that govern meaning.* Become more aware of factors that shape collective meaning and nurture history, stories, visions, inquiries, beliefs, education, experiences and values that help people relate more fully to those around them, to nature, and to the future.

- *Healthy physical contexts.* Become more aware of physical environments and nurture settings that support people's life energy—taking into account spaces, resources, distances, infrastructure, timing and pacing, and relative comfort, stress, and physical safety.

- *Healthy natural contexts.* Become more aware of the presence and condition of nonhuman beings and systems. Nurture healthy natural environments, systems, processes, resources, and living beings including animals, plants, fungi and bacteria. Nurture a mutual, sustainable human relationship with them. Take only what nature can afford to give, and deliver into natural systems only what they can readily absorb and use.

3. Cultivate healthy systemic responsiveness and collective evolvability. Evolution naturally favors living systems that can coherently interact with their changing environments, and can change themselves when necessary. Responsiveness is the primary evolutionary rationale for consciousness. Evolutionary activists promote institutions that enable whole human systems—from households to global economic systems—to take initiatives and respond in ways that sustain a healthy relationship (fit) with their changing circumstances (Atlee, 2003). Here are some approaches that contribute to collective evolvability and responsiveness, each of which includes examples with references, or which you can research further on the Web:

- *Cultivate collective intelligence, learning, and memory* - from Open Space (Owen, 1997) and World Café (Brown, 2005) conferences and media reform to Wikipedia and cooperative education

- *Cultivate collective self-awareness, integrity, and humility* - from the Precautionary Principle and annual Wisdom Councils (Rough, 2002), to legal protections for whistle blowers and reading foreign news commentaries about our own country

- *Cultivate the collective capacity to generate and pursue shared intentions* - from scenario planning and community vision programs, to social networking sites and Future Search Conferences (Weisbord and Janoff, 2000)

- *Cultivate systems that embody collective compassion and mutuality* - from universal health care and truth and reconciliation commissions, to community supported agriculture and local currencies

- *Cultivate the collective ability to make wise, creative decisions* - from citizen deliberative councils and the Earth Charter process, to the Genuine Progress Indicator and electoral reform (Atlee, 2003; Crosby, 2003; Gastil, 2000)

- *Cultivate collective co-creativity and evolutionary sensibilities* - from shared novel-writing and Storyfield Conferences, to co-creating evolutionary spirituality and movies about evolutionary activists

References

Alexander, Christopher: *A Pattern Language* (Oxford, 1977).

Atlee, Tom: *The Tao of Democracy: Using co-intelligence to create a world that works for all* (Writers Collective, 2003).

Benyus, Janine M.: *Innovation Inspired by Nature* (Harper Perennial, 2002).

Brown, Juanita and David Isaacs: *World Cafe* (Berrett-Koehler, 2005).

Crosby, Ned: *Healthy Democracy* (Beaver's Pond Press, 2003).

Dowd, Michael: *Thank God for Evolution* (Viking Penguin, 2008).

Ecotrust: *A Pattern Language for a Conservation Economy: What Does a Sustainable Society Look Like?* (c.2000) at conservationeconomy.net.

Gardner, Howard: *Frames of Mind* (Basic Books, 1983).

Gastil, John: *By Popular Demand: Revitalizing Representative Democracy Through Deliberative Elections* (University of California, 2000).

Hawken, Paul, Amory Lovins, L. Hunter Lovins: *Natural Capitalism* (Back Bay, 2000).

Henderson, Hazel: *Paradigms in Progress: Life Beyond Economics* (Knowledge Systems, 1991).

Holman, Peggy, Tom Devane and Steven Cady: *The Change Handbook* (Berrett-Koehler, 2007).

Korten, David: *The Great Turning* (Berrett-Koehler, 2006).

Kreuzer, Michael Jr.: *This View of Life: A Beginner's Guide to a Science-Based Understanding of Evolution* (thisviewoflife.org/ecology/energy.html, Mar 2007).

Mollison, Bill: *Permaculture: A Practical Guide for a Sustainable Future* (Island Press, 1990).

Owen, Harrison: *Open Space Technology: A User's Guide* (Berrett-Koehler, 1997).

Rough, Jim: *Society's Breakthrough! Releasing Essential Wisdom and Virtue in All the People* (1stBooks, 2002).

Weisbord, Marvin and Sandra Janoff: *Future Search* (Berrett-Koehler, 2000).

Together at the Leading Edge

The leading edge exists for each of us
and for all of us
right in front of us
just beyond what we already know.

Like the horizon,
every where is the leading edge
for someone, somewhere.
The leading edge is a moving target.

Each of us
of course can only know what we know
and work with that,
going beyond
to learn.

But how do we know what we know together?
And how do we work with that, together,
going beyond it, to learn
at the leading edge
together?

When "going beyond" is where it's at,
what is a "mistake"?

What is "failure"?
Where do we find success?
What are we afraid of?
What is "good enough"
at any given time
when we're together
at the leading edge?

Rumi says that
beyond right and wrong
there is a field:
he'll meet you there.

I say that beyond knowing and unknowing
there is a field.
I sort of know where it is, and sort of don't.
I'd like to look for it with you, exploring
and discovering, over and over again,
that we've been here all along.

At the leading edge,
everything we think we know
is a place to leap from
which, if we don't leap,
becomes a chain around our legs,
a blindfold on our eyes,

and starts to dissolve below our feet
so we have to leap anyway,
hobbled and blindfolded.

The wisdom we seek
is to learn to leap together
pushed, prodded, guided, encouraged, partnered,
by one another
into more than we saw
into more than we knew
moment to moment
in more dimensions than any of us can ever comprehend
forever.

There is no preparation for this.
Everything we've ever done is preparation for this.
Perhaps there is something to know
about doing this elegantly.
But no one can teach it
because every teaching is another chain,
     another blindfold,
unless we leap.

Isn't this what we're doing?
Even when we think we're doing everything else?

| ✳ |

Chapter Twenty-Three

Five areas to attend to when building an evolutionary activism movement

INDIVIDUAL DEVELOPMENT AND ENGAGEMENT: Efforts to expand individual consciousness, mind, heart, and will to perceive and embrace the evolution and wellbeing of the whole. This includes meditation, education, community programs, personal transformation, evolutionary religious forms, action support networks, and ways to inform and engage people in evolution as a meaningful story and enterprise that includes them as active participants.

COLLECTIVE KNOWING: Projects that free, increase, and empower collective consciousness, intelligence, and wisdom. This includes ways for whole communities and societies to clearly see what's happening in and around them, and their past, present, and future role in that. Keys to this include improved media and other storytelling, effective methods of collective reflection, and compelling evolutionary arts.

STRATEGIC CONVERSATIONS: Activities that identify where conversation would make a powerful difference in our collective prospects for evolutionary development—and then creatively bring together diverse, relevant viewpoints or developmental threads so they can evolve together into more consciously co-creative undertakings. This includes networking individuals and groups, small focused dialogues, and various large-scale gatherings and conferences around topics, issues, possibilities, or open-ended evolutionary inquiries.

SOCIAL RESPONSIBILITY AND ENLIGHTENED SELF-INTEREST: Laws and culture through which people and organizations experience for themselves the positive and negative impacts they cause on others and on the whole (e.g., the whole community, society, or world). This includes anything that aligns the day-to-day self-interest of individual entities with the real and evolutionary interests of the whole, including economic incentives, regulatory and chartering constraints, and cultural celebrations, narratives, and taboos. This is basically a reworking of the cultural feedback loops that govern human behavior so they serve humanity's collective survival and healthy evolution.

RESEARCH AND DEVELOPMENT: All these evolutionary enterprises require (a) the gathering, orienting and spreading of existing know-how, stories, and resources; (b) the development of more powerful understandings and tools than currently exist to pursue their aims; (c) the development of means whereby these enterprises can observe themselves, learn lessons from their collective experience, and transform themselves; and (d) the creation of forums whereby individuals, groups, communities, organizations, etc., can self-organize increasingly effective evolutionary research and development of their own.

Sun being meditation

The Sun has been churning out energy
in all directions—
more energy than we can comprehend
in all directions—
for billions of years.

We, 93,000,000 miles away,
have been soaking up
a mere four billionths of all that energy.

And from that minuscule fraction
of the Sun's eons of churning
has come all the wind
and all the rain
and the magic of photosynthesis
and thus
practically every motion
by every organism
since the beginning of life.

And so we find that every act of life
for over three billion years
is a direct manifestation
of the Earth's loving bond with the Sun.

My writing this
is a solar event.
Your reading it
is a solar event.

Take another breath, sunshine.
You are all that is, around here.

| ✳ |

Chapter Twenty-Four

Imagining an activist movement for the conscious evolution of social systems

What would a conscious evolutionary activist movement look like? I'll share my thoughts here, more as a stimulant to dialogue than as a prescription or prediction.

From my current understanding and inclinations, I believe:

> **A conscious evolutionary activist movement**
> **would choose to play an active part in evolution,**
> **helping humanity (and itself) move consciously**
> **towards evolutionary fitness and**
> **elegantly functional self-organized complexity.**

As I sense into this visionary definition, I see many interesting components and corollaries. I want to explore them here by imagining what those of us who are attracted to this vision might do with them. Let's assume for a moment that we have such a movement, and look at what we are doing in it and with it....

> *First of all, I see us studying and being guided by evolutionary dynamics—the process dynamics of nature. This is not a sideline. It is as essential to us as studying the medical literature is to a good doctor or studying the Bible is to an evangelical Christian. We are reading evolutionary literature to find out and share all we can about all the evolutionary dynamics that have been going on for almost 14 billion years—noticing how those dynamics themselves evolve as they go.*
>
> *What evolutionary dynamics can be used to transform social systems? We are not only all students of this question, but we collectively support and participate in real research into this new field of investigation (for example, by participating in the evolutionary spirituality wiki[16]). For any and all evolutionary dynamics, we discuss how it applies to our circumstances, and how we might carry it into its own next evolutionary step. As conscious evolutionaries, we are aware that evolution itself is evolving its dynamics through our learning and action, and we engage in that work as an active duty, an exercise in conscious evolution.*
>
> *Near the top of our list, I see us trying to understand how to most creatively use differences and disturbances— including the major crises of our time—as evolutionary doorways—and also how to align diverse self-interests with*

---

[16] evolutionaryspirituality.wikia.com

the wellbeing of the whole. (My investigations so far have led me to believe those two evolutionary principles contain most of the guidance we need. Heaven knows, we already have tons of opportunities to experiment in these areas alone!)

Although grounded in science, our explorations are not a merely rational exercise. For many of us, intuition, imagination, aesthetics, and physical involvement play vital roles in our learning and discovery processes. Furthermore, most of us evolutionary activists find the science valuable only to the extent it excites and inspires us, giving us clarity and a sense that we're not just pushing an agenda or following a formula, but participating as knowledgable apprentices with nature in a profoundly important undertaking it has been working on since the beginning of time. We become parts of what Ursula Goodenough calls "the sacred depths of nature". This is not primarily a rational task, although reason and facts are among our most valued sources of understanding.

Even though we are activists, we are not only working on evolving what's outside of us. In fact, we have our own versions of the self-development and human potential activities that are widespread in the "conscious evolution" subculture. Our versions embrace any and all practices from that subculture—particularly where each of us finds personal value in such practices. In addition, we are especially attentive to the personal developmental challenges and opportunities that accompany our activism. This is part of our activism.

We know that when we take action to change a system, the system tends to resist, to push back. That is natural. Systems need to have that habit in order to remain coherent, to hold their form and identity—in short, in order to survive. But they also need to be flexible, which is where we come in. As evolutionary activists, we know that we have to work WITH the push-back we get from the systems we are trying to change. We see such push-back as a sign both of something that needs to change and as a source of life energy and guidance as we catalyze the needed changes.

In close affinity groups we act together and support our own evolution

We also know that social systems aren't the only systems that push back. Just as we bump up against resistances in the world, so we bump up against them in and among ourselves. So in our movement activities, we constantly test ourselves and discover ways we need to—and can—learn, expand and shift. Most of us are involved in intimate, often local support groups, fellowships and networks that support us AS ACTIVISTS in working on our own evolution—and on our ability to function well together—as well as on the evolution of society's systems and cultures. In spiritual terms, we arrange things so that our activism is actually a spiritual practice, just as Service or Love are spiritual paths in many existing religions, or like Truth was for Gandhi or Love for Martin Luther King, Jr.

Of course as a force for evolution we have no desire for a movement that is static and ideological. Not only would that not be "walking our talk," but it would be an active impediment to our mission. So we are eager collective learners and becoming masters of appropriate shape-shifting to meet changing demands and opportunities. We try to weave our movement out of inclusive ecosystems of diverse, interrelated ideas, strategies, tactics, media, people, and organizing forms.

In our efforts to be intelligently inclusive—to be integral—we ask questions like "What are the gifts and limitations of this?" and "Where does this fit in relation to everything else?" and "What is possible now?" Whenever we stumble into blame and arguing about whether something is right or wrong, we do what we can to shift to this other level of inclusive possibility thinking.

Our movement has emerged and is evolving itself through such conscious interactions and co-creativity in active response to changing conditions in and around it. We engage in a tremendous amount of juicy conversation. It is productive conversation, neither inspiring nor deserving the "all talk and no action" critique so common years ago. Our talking is guided by a pioneering intention that we need, perhaps above all, to learn how to do powerful conversations well, for they are the medium through which our cooperation, our collective learning, and our co-creativity can change the world. So we usually reflect on our conversations before, during, and after them in an effort to learn how to do them better.

Our attention is focused on the social systems, cultures, consciousness and technology that generate the life-

enhancing and life-degrading things that happen in our world. We recognize that we are not outside of them, nor are we the only actors, nor can we accomplish what's needed by ourselves, no matter how numerous we are. Our approach is always to look for where the energy for creative shift is — no matter how faint or strange it may seem — and to support it to develop in ways that will assist the larger society's motion to become more sustainable and life-enhancing. We look for ways to access the wisdom of the whole in service of the whole — using advances in democracy, conversation, technology, collaboration, spirituality, cognition, story... We look for the acupuncture points where a small intervention will tap the tremendous evolutionary energies latent in all out-of-equilibrium situations and systems, and together we attend to what happens when we act at that point, and learn from our experience. We know we are not creating a new culture. We are helping a civilization become capable of creating itself wisely, over and over, and we enjoy the sacred mystery of how to do that and how it all unfolds. We are part of the Great Learning.

Of course, none of this will play out the way it does on paper here. It will play out in a dance with whatever we do, with things happening because we are conscious of them and things happening because we *aren't* conscious of them. We will learn how to become more conscious about what we *need* to be conscious of and more insightful, courageous, and elegant in how we act on that. At the same time, we will always let the larger body of life carry us in grace and mystery, teaching us as it goes. That is, after all, what this is all about.

To Martin Luther King, Jr.

I have a dream
that We the People—
  that elusive mythic power
  that is our one linked life—
will awaken from the nightmare
where we willingly,   unwaryingly,
subserve our will and our sun-varied lives
and our pricelessly unspun future
  to Powers so hungrily brilliant
    that we think we serve ourselves
    when we serve our colonized
    lives, desires, minds
      to their hunger.

I have a dream, deep beyond forgetting,
that We the People—
  the spirit power at the core
  of one and All—
will awaken into heart and thought woven
with the invisible Power of the Universe,
with the all-pervasive powers of life,
and with our own blessedly multiplicitous

powers of sight and bold gesture,
  to make a world so alive
  with such wisdom, energy and joy
that dreaming living dreams
on behalf of the best life has to offer
    becomes the grand golden loom
      upon which a new wisely beloved civilization
gets woven with ourselves and our children.

And in my dream, deep in the dawn
of yestermorrow's rains
blessed in the dust of our lives,
one and All reclaim
our seeing, our life, and our time —
and one another, first of all —
and on that stardust stage
between the deepening nightmare
  where waking
    never comes
and the dream of a gateway world
  where waking
    goes on forever,
we turn, and together wake
and a bluebright day floods in.

| ✳ |

Chapter Twenty-Five

Some ways to engage in co-creating this movement

All of the links here, and indeed from throughout the book, are available online at evolutionaryactivism.com. *In addition, I'll be adding activities and resources there that have emerged after this edition of the book is published. If you know of other evolutionary activist resources or activities, email me at cii@igc.org with "Evolutionary Activism Activities" as the subject. Contact me if you have questions or comments, especially if you would like to engage in this new kind of activist movement, the creation of which is the entire purpose of this book.*

At the time of this writing, many thousands of activists are doing work that fits the strategic perspective described here, without thinking of their work in evolutionary terms. Meanwhile, thousands of conscious evolutionary agents are doing *their* work without thinking about it through this kind of strategic activist perspective. We are just beginning to bring people from these groups together in a coherent strategic vision of evolutionary activism. I invite you to become part of the launching of this activist branch of the conscious evolution movement—or the conscious evolutionary branch of various existing activist movements.

There are many things you can do. Here are some initial thoughts:

1. Take action from this evolutionary perspective.
Begin, continue, and support efforts to change social systems, technology, or culture in ways that will serve our evolution into a sustainable, wisely self-evolving civilization.

2. Build communities and networks around evolutionary activism.
Connect with friends, colleagues and others on- and offline to support each other in learning about and living evolutionary activism. Share this book and other sources referenced below. Get together to explore this and related subjects. Support one another in taking action. My own views on what counts as evolutionary activism are spread throughout this book and my book *The Tao of Democracy* covers much of the political vision in far greater detail, although without framing it as

evolutionary. Develop and share your own views on this topic. My books are only a beginning and/or a resource.

If you'd like to co-organize action from this perspective, and/or share and explore your own and others' views and experiences, here are several opportunities to participate:

a. **Evolutionary Activism listserv**

> *groups.yahoo.com/group/EvolutionaryActivism*
> or just email
> *EvolutionaryActivism-subscribe@groups.yahoo.com*

For discussing evolutionary action, ideas, questions, issues, current events, and more.

b. **Evolutionary Spirituality Wiki**

> *evolutionaryspirituality.wikia.com*

An open space for us to explore and co-organize this movement together. I'll probably also work on and invite collaboration there on a second edition of this book, or a new book especially for activists unfamiliar with the evolutionary perspective.

c. **Phone conference calls and workshops**

Check *evolutionaryactivism.com* for announcements about these. We use *maestropath.com*, a service which allows dozens or even hundreds of people to participate, and use their own phone key pad to vote or 'raise their hands' to speak; it also lets us create breakout groups in World Cafe or perhaps even Open Space formats -- all on the phone.

d. Track news from me

If you'd like to hear more from me on evolutionary activism and related subjects, follow my blog "Random Communications from an Evolutionary Edge" at *tom-atlee.posterous.com*, and / or my Twitter feed at *twitter.com/tomatlee*

e. Share your news and resources with me and each other

If you know of or create an in-person group, or a blog or social networking group (or an entire service!) that is enthusiastic about evolutionary activism, let me know and I'll publicize it and / or join you there. When there's exciting news from your group or blog, please let me know about that as well. My hope is that in the long run other coordinators will emerge to facilitate the flow of information, on the Evolutionary Spirituality wiki or by other means, so that I don't become a bottleneck for our collective organizing.

Join in co-creating
an evolutionary activist movement!

3. Learn more about the Great Story, Big History, evolutionary spirituality, and evolutionary dynamics—and how we can apply them to transforming social systems. As a start, I recommend five books, all of which are themselves rich sources and have excellent bibliographies and/or notes to guide further reading:

- Brian Swimme and Thomas Berry: *The Universe Story*
- Michael Dowd: *Thank God for Evolution*
- David Sloan Wilson: *Evolution for Everyone*
- Robert Wright: *NonZero*
- John Stewart: *Evolution's Arrow*

4. Support this work financially through Evolutionary Life. Send a fully tax-deductible contribution to

Evolutionary Life
PO Box 10374
Eugene, OR 97440

or go online to

evolutionarylife.com/Donate.html

Finally, as you educate yourself about this emerging perspective and movement, stay connected to your inner passions, longings, and dreams for the world. Thinking about leverage is important, but it is only the rational twin of a more powerful source of energy and guidance, your own sense of calling. As best as you can, pursue your own current best answer to, "Where do my gifts and passions meet the world's evolutionary need at this time?" Your answer will evolve as you learn about evolution, observe what's happening in the world, participate in evolutionary activist networks, and stay grounded in what calls you from the inside, which is connected to the Whole, the Creative Power of the Universe.

Blessings on the Journey.

Co-aliveness

Life weaves
Life breathes
Life seethes
with Life
within us, around us,
over us, under us,
into us, out of us,
all of us dancing,
dancing, dancing, dancing.

One in the world
and the world in one
and the ferns unfurled
in the soothing Sun
And all of us living
dreaming strands
of fabric streaming
from the hands
of co-aliveness,
co-aliveness,
co-aliveness dancing.

The fruits that pop
into a crop
of seeds that drop
to earth don't stop...
But wars and malls
and sufferings
will be transformed
to other things
by co-aliveness,
co-aliveness,
co-aliveness dancing.

There's so much more
that we could say,
for tomorrow's sure
of another day
where the ocean shore
will find its way
through an open door
of an endless play
of co-aliveness,
co-aliveness,
co-aliveness dancing.

Life weaves
Life breathes
Life seethes
with Life
within us, around us,
over us, under us,
into us, out of us,
all of us dancing,
dancing, dancing, dancing.

| ✳ |

Appendices

Appendix A

An annotated informal glossary
of basic terms

Complexity: Complexity is not about *complicatedness*. It is about dense interconnection, co-creative interactivity, and mutual interdependence among diverse entities. It comes about in layers (some say a hierarchy), as when atoms make a molecule or cells make a body or people make a community. At each stage, parts make up a whole that has a coherence and qualities of its own. A complex whole is, when seen as a whole, a simple entity. But the closer you look, the more detailed parts and interconnections you find. This is also true of a situation, problem, reality, ecosystem, and so on. A major challenge to humanity at this stage is to be able to tolerate, comprehend, and work with the complexity of our situation, while developing more elegantly complex (coherently and functionally interactive) social systems and worldviews. Complexity also refers to the non-linear dynamics of complex systems—from societies to climate systems—and the scientific study of those systems, as well as the participatory, probability-based worldview suggested by the science of complexity.

Consciousness: By consciousness I mean the capacity to be aware, and the qualities, contents, and manifestations of our awareness and minds, individually and collectively. This includes phenomena like:
- responsiveness, intentionality, and intelligence
- the stories we tell ourselves and others (or are told)
- the beliefs and values we hold and how we hold them
- the ways we learn or become aware (or don't), individually and collectively—and *what* we know or are aware of
- the level of wisdom and insight we are capable of, and our arrogance or humility about what we know
- the way we view challenges, dissonance, crises, etc.
- the openness of our hearts and minds.

For more, see *co-intelligence.org/Consciousness.html*

Conscious evolution means becoming an aware, intentional participant in the evolutionary process. Conscious evolution means seeking to be aware of what is involved in the process of evolution in specific domains and situations. And it means seeking to be aware of who we are and who we might be in relation to this process. It involves making choices and taking action—or not—with as much awareness as we can of our evolutionary role as we seek to serve and manifest the best of what life is and seeks to be. Conscious evolution means not only being a conscious agent of evolution, but also realizing we are living manifestations of that aspect of evolution that is becoming conscious of itself.

Dissonance: For an evolutionary activist, dissonance marks the rough leading edge of evolution that is calling our attention to itself and demanding our creative engagement. Dissonance includes disagreement, disturbance, strangeness, edgy fringes, discomfort, suffering, problems, crisis, challenges, visions, passions, destruction, confusion, failure, loss, threat, death, conflict, and anything else that pulls us out of business as usual, shakes up existing structures and patterns, or makes us want to turn away, or provokes us to actively engage with what is emerging or suppressed. While there are limits to how much dissonance any entity or system can tolerate, from an evolutionary perspective, those limits exist to be stretched and transcended.

Evolution: In its generic sense, evolution is progressive change or development. In this book we see it as the process through which reality has unfolded in increasing complexity for 13.7 billion years—moving from energy to quarks to atoms to molecules to objects, to organisms and societies, through cosmic evolution, stellar evolution, geological evolution, biological evolution, cultural evolution, technological evolution, and the evolution of consciousness and social systems. Each of these evolutionary "phase changes" created entirely new realms in which evolutionary dynamics could play out and themselves evolve. With the emergence of conscious evolution—evolution through wise choice—we find ourselves in one more entirely new evolutionary realm.

System: By system I mean a dynamic, interactive array of elements and relationships that sustains itself over time. A system's elements and relationships shape the whole system and the system as a whole shapes the elements and relationships that make it up. (Thus the same element in a different system would have different qualities and impacts.) Although natural systems (ecosystems, chemical cycles, climate systems, etc.) are vital and occasionally mentioned in this book, evolutionary activists tend to focus on **social systems** like

- political and governmental systems
- economic and financial systems
- intelligence, information, and knowledge systems (from journalism to education to the CIA to the Internet)
- food, transportation, and energy systems
- technological systems (the interrelated technologies we use to do things)
- cultural and worldview systems composed of narratives, assumptions, and the collective structures and behaviors that manifest and reinforce them.

Wholeness: By wholeness I mean the inclusive, ever-evolving coherence (a) of life and its various parts and (b) of the relationship dynamics between those parts. This coherence underlies familiar concepts like health, integrity, wholesomeness, holiness, and other holistic concepts. Reality is always a coherent whole, while containing aspects that are in dynamic tension with other aspects, stimulating interactions and emergences that resolve those dynamic tensions while, at the same time, creating tensions in other parts of the whole. This cycle of tension, resolution, tension, etc., results in the phenomenon of evolving wholeness, a basic guiding principle of evolutionary activism. In practice, wholeness involves

- nurturing and using our whole selves and our whole collectivity

- engaging the whole situation and all the players, most notably any dissonance, disturbance, problems, longings, and other forms of friction with the status quo

- taking into account all parts of the big picture, including deep time (the long-view past, the long-view future, and the full present) and the multifaceted complexity of any given situation (which involves a certain amount of humility and capacitance—the ability to tolerate paradox, dissonance, ambiguity and uncertainty)

- acknowledging broad spectrum evolutionary dynamics, including multi-level selection that operates simultaneously in genetic and social realms

- promoting all that is healthy, holy, wholesome, healing, inclusive, and synergistic

- and a whole lot more.

The more of the whole of anything we consider or welcome as a resource or call into being, the more wholeness manifests. This century challenges us to become more whole, to heal our world, and to create healthy societies that can delight in and use the richness and vitality of human wholeness in conscious context with the wholeness of the world we live in. For more see *co-intelligence.org/I-wholeness.html.*

Appendix B

Evolutionary Life

Evolutionary Life *evolutionarylife.com* is a 501(c)(3) non-profit organization formed to promote more effective conscious evolutionary understandings and activities. Its foundational beliefs and purpose are as follows:

We believe

a. that humanity is a part and expression of the Great Story of universal evolution,

b. that humanity represents the possibility of evolution becoming conscious of itself and

c. that the extent to which humanity takes the leap into conscious evolution will determine humanity's existence and quality of life during the 21st century and thereafter.

We believe that inspired conscious evolutionary behavior can be an everyday experience and that humanity is limited largely by its perceptions of the story it is living. We intend to help humanity expand into consciousness of its role in the great evolutionary story so that, rather than destroying itself, it can progressively live into its most life-serving possibilities.

We nurture humanity's evolutionary role in three fundamental areas:
- learning, research, and teaching the reality and dynamics of evolution
- celebration, support, and community—grounded in the spirit of evolution
- practice, service, and transformational action that embodies evolution at all levels—personal, social systemic, and planetary.

Fully tax-deductible contributions are welcomed and can be sent to

Evolutionary Life
PO Box 10374
Eugene, OR 97440

or online go to
evolutionarylife.com/Donate.html

Appendix C

Models of transformational leverage

Presented here are several different, but overlapping, models to stimulate our thinking about where and how we can have the most impact. You will find the basic thrust of them summarized in Chapter 13 "Transformational leverage."

Model #1 - Targets of intervention

HIGHEST LEVERAGE INTERVENTIONS: Increasing the *capacity of the society* to function in positive ways and, especially, to change itself (consciously evolve) in positive directions. This involves shifts—often systemic—in

- **consciousness** (awareness, assumptions, attitude, story)
- **community** and relationships (including power relationships and social capital)
- **conversation** and deliberation
- **capacity** for collective intelligence, collective response, and collective initiative

- **systems** or patterns of activity (habits, institutions, structures, practices, economic indicators, feedback loops), infrastructure, subsidiarity, decision-making systems, resource allocation—especially availability of resources for self-organization
- **technology,** particularly when it is based on natural patterns or it impacts people's modes of interactivity.

MEDIUM LEVERAGE INTERVENTIONS: Making incremental changes in society's functionality, changing

- **laws,** policies, regulations, and programs (in ways that don't fundamentally change the high leverage factors above)
- **incentives** and the behaviors related to those incentives
- **powerholders** (corporate leaders, elected officials, role models).

LOW LEVERAGE INTERVENTIONS: Dealing with the *effects* of society's obsolete and dysfunctional activities. This involves changing

- **conditions** (e.g. poverty, suffering, toxic dumps, disasters)
- **locations** (e.g., moving problems from one time and place to another—e.g, NIMBY)
- **events** (e.g., stopping a war or clearcut).

We can consider these last action targets lower-leverage because new forms of these problems will continue to surface if the systems that help bring them about or sustain them continue.

Model #2: Strategies

Here is another way to cut the leverage pie, more focused on actions than on targets of action:

LOW LEVERAGE STRATEGIES

1. *Ameliorating* individual or group suffering, injustice or threat
2. *Stopping* bad things from happening (war, pollution, cancer, discrimination, etc.)
3. *Promoting* pet solutions, projects, ideas, or issues in isolation from others

HIGHER LEVERAGE STRATEGIES (these overlap in important ways, but have distinct "centers" of their own)

1. *Building a wiser democracy*—This tackles perhaps the core issue: How (and how well) decisions are made on *all* issues. This includes local, national and global power relationships; public dialogue (including process and information access issues); and institutions for wise decision-making, among other things.

2. *Transforming cultural assumptions*—This is the paradigm shift, the change of worldviews. Cultural assumptions inform the underlying structures that determine how people think and respond. Change these assumptions and you have changed everything else, all at once. We want to move society's assumptions towards holistic, multi-level, collaborative, ecological, evolutionary, and living-systems perspectives.

3. *Developing and promoting sustainable technologies*—Technology affects how people do things and, by itself, creates social change. Three archetypes of society-changing technologies (that too often move us in the "wrong" direction) are the car, TV and computer. When the word "sustainable" is used, most people think environmentally friendly technologies. This sustainable technologies strategy includes those, but also human technologies for collaboration, collective learning, and self-organization, all of which are vital for a sustainable culture. Getting all of them used is at least as important as having them available. Related to this is:

4. *Building human capacity*—both individual and collective. The challenges humans face are immense. The human potential movement did much to enhance our ability to embrace, process and address challenges, but primarily at an individual

level. We need a comparable program to increase our *collective* capacity for the same, particularly (a) among groups, organizations, networks and coalitions working for positive social transformation and evolution, (b) in communities of place, practice, and purpose, and (c) in society as a whole.

5. *Improving resources for transformation*—Part of improving these resources is channeling existing resources towards transformation. Another part of it is getting smarter about how to get more for less (e.g., through the intelligent use of creativity, design for self-organization, synergy, and community). The transformation of philanthropy is a priority because the overwhelming majority of financial resources are held by the top 10% of people in most societies. Another aspect is helping "movement" groups and organizations co-create an evolving shared coherence—networks, strategies, visions, best practices, common ground, activist culture, evolutionary perspective, etc.

6. *Using diversity and crises as resources*—This includes and transcends the usual diversity and conflict work, which are often based on problematic relationships of power and privilege. Differences and crises are powerful medicine:

They can be an incredible resource or a devastating obstacle, depending on how they are used. This leverage strategy is focused on tapping into the power of diversity and crises in ways that permanently transform people's awareness, attitudes, relationships, and skills, and/ or change the field within which people interact, so that human differences, conflicts, and crises are recognized as having the capacity to shake up the status quo, thereby offering opportunity, insight, energy, and talents for transformation and evolution.

7. *Impeding totalistic threats*—This is the only high-leverage strategy that tries to stop something. What it stops is genocidal activities (the destruction of species, cultures, languages) and omnicidal technologies (such as certain biotech developments that could destroy all life or human life) from which recovery may be impossible. Bill Joy's April 2000 *Wired* article "Why the Future Doesn't Need Us" and the current terrorist threat combine to wake us up to the fact that soon individuals or small groups will be empowered to effectively "destroy the world" accidentally or intentionally. Sudden climate change also presents such a threat. Preventing such disasters may only be possible with real progress on the other strategies.

Model #3: Collective learning

Every one of the above strategies demands learning, not just by individuals, but by everyone, and/or by collective living systems—organizations, communities, societies—acting as intelligent living agents in their own right. We need to be extremely clear about how to enhance this learning capacity and use it with focused intent. Among the collective learning tools we might improve or transform, and use to further all the transformational strategies above, are the following. At least one example is included with each tool. Further information regarding these examples is available on the Web.

A. *Education* - education in systems thinking

B. *Media* - expanding civic journalism; Journalism that Matters

C. *Societal feedback loops* - such as citizen deliberative councils, which reflect back to citizens the wisdom they could discover if they all had sufficient time, information, and opportunities for dialogue with one another

D. *Story* - like the women's movement having women share their stories; communities creating a shared vision together; storyfield conferences

E. *Research* - such as experiments that demonstrate that (and how) people with diverse values can work together co-creatively and effectively on public issues

F. *Statistics* (a powerful form of collective/systemic perception) - for example, replacing GDP with Quality of Life indicators

G. *Marketing* - e.g., placing transformational messages in popular movies; culture jamming

H. *The Arts* - for example, broadcasting performances which embody diverse perspectives on public issues or events (for example, Anna Deavere Smith's one-woman shows).

I. *Best practices* - e.g., establishing websites for the sharing of what works and doesn't in communities and activism

J. *Dialogue* (I believe this one is most important) - for example, providing citizens chosen for their diversity with excellent facilitation and information to make recommendations on public issues (see C, above), and having those recommendations circulated to study circles around the country for discussion; also, strategic conversations convened among specific stakeholders to realize targeted potential or release targeted stuck energy

K. *Innovation diffusion* - Recently there have been studies of how innovations spread through a society, which is a form of societal learning, e.g., *The Tipping Point* by Malcolm Gladwell.

> *Reminder: Most of the above collective learning*
> *tools are applicable to all of the 1-7 strategies, and*
> *can themselves be considered interrelated, medium-*
> *to-high leverage targets for improvement.*

Model #4: A "modes of intervention" ladder

In this hierarchical model, each mode of intervention includes and reaches beyond the mode(s) below it—thus the metaphor of a ladder. An evolutionary catalyst at the top of the ladder would tend to use all the other modes, but selectively at particularly ripe times (e.g., a crisis), to help the existing players and energies in the system make an evolutionary leap in a healthy direction. In general, as leaders, evolutionaries, philanthropists, activists, and other social change agents intervene higher on the ladder, they tend to produce more leverage for evolutionary transformation.

1. **Evolutionary catalytic action.** Tweaking the evolutionary *process* in a social system, especially at crisis points, especially in ways that enhance the system's collective intelligence and wisdom

2. **Social shamanism.** Working[17] the context, culture, story, paradigm, goal, field, etc., within which a social system operates

---

[17] "Working" here refers to following and engaging in transformational ways with the larger patterns that shape a system. It is a sensitive, responsive form of purposefulness, as when a potter "works the clay."

3. **Social systems design.** Designing and reworking overall systems and feedback dynamics

4. **Servant leadership.** Designing and empowering networks and communities; building capacity for self-organization in specific realms

5. **Process artistry.** Hosting generative interactions among a social system's diverse players, stakeholders, leaders, etc.

6. **Activism.** Mobilizing concerned citizens and victims around specific causes and candidates to change conditions

7. **Education.** Giving people the information and training they need to help themselves as individuals and as groups

8. **Charity.** Helping individuals and groups directly

9. **Sympathy.** Knowing and resonating with another's suffering or telling other people about suffering that exists.

A final personal observation and inquiry

Things are changing fast, even as I write this and you read it. Changing our own ways of dealing with our work, or relations with one another, and the forms of support we need and give, is essential if we are to be able to respond and initiate in timely, appropriate fashions. This is a form of capacity-building.

But none of us has enough time. I suspect if we handled that—for most social problems are tied to that "no time" dynamic, one way or another—we'd be half way home...

What do we put our attention on?

NOTE: Evolutionary activists may also wish to study Donella Meadows' famous essay "Leverage Points: Places to intervene in a system" *sustainer.org/pubs/Leverage_Points.pdf.*

Index

About the author

Tom Atlee is founder of the Co-Intelligence Institute, co-founder of Evolutionary Life, and author of *The Tao of Democracy: Using Co-Intelligence to Create a World that Works for All*, as well as dozens of articles for alternative journals. Coming from a traditional progressive activist background, he became interested in how to develop the wisdom of whole communities and societies and, more recently, in how to further the conscious evolution of humanity and its social systems and cultures. He lives in Eugene, OR and can be contacted at cii@igc.org.

Websites associated with Tom Atlee's work:
- *co-intelligence.org*
- *evolutionarylife.com*
- *taoofdemocracy.com*
- *tom-atlee.posterous.com* (blog)
- *evolutionaryactivism.com*

Acknowledgments

I wish to express my deepest gratitude for

- my parents, John and Elinore Atlee, for my initiation in this lifetime, for raising me with a social conscience, with a sense of agency and urgency, with systemic and evolutionary awareness, and with a real love for democracy
- my daughter, Jennifer Atlee, for her strong support in the creation of this book, for her partnership in my heart and at the leading edge of my thinking, and for her profound teachings in deep ecology
- my brother, Dick Atlee, for his persistent support and belief in my work and in me, no matter how hopeless our situation seemed to him
- my fellow board members (past and present) of the Co-Intelligence Institute and Evolutionary Life who have constantly re-established the ground I stand on and shared my wild sense of possibility—Adin Rogovin, Lyn Bazzell, Heather Tischbein, John Abbe, Karen Mercer, Elliot Shuford, Susan Edwards, Eileen Palmer, Miki Kashtan, Kevin Reidy,

Mary Ann Gallagher, Peggy Holman and Susan Cannon. I want to especially thank John Abbe for his help working out this book's post-publication program of conversation and connection, and for his help on the cover.

- Michael Dowd and Connie Barlow for introducing me to the sacred evolutionary worldview, for triggering my evolutionary epiphany, and for their ongoing companionship and many forms of encouragement and help on this Great Journey

- Peggy Holman for her dedicated friendship and creative engagement exploring with me the useful edges of evolutionary wisdom in catalyzing social change, for sharing her brilliant thinking on emergence, and for teaching me so much about the power of nonlinear conversational fields

- the many evolutionary agents and writers of all kinds who have created the evolutionary subculture within which I swim, and from which I get such tremendous nourishment, inspiration, and challenge—most especially among them Brian Swimme, David Spangler, Barbara Marx Hubbard, Susan Cannon, Robert Wright, Joshua Gorman, John Stewart, Elisabet Sahtouris, Peter Corning, David Sloan Wilson, David Christian, Joel Primack, Nancy Ellen Abrams, Ken Wilber, Don Beck, Paul Ehrlich, Robert Ornstein, Duane Elgin, Andrew Cohen, Jean Houston, Joanna

Macy, evolutionary networker Sheri Herndon, and evolutionary activist poets Drew Dellinger and Vanessa German—to name just a few!

- the W.K. Kellogg Foundation and its former inspired, pioneering program officer Guillermina Hernandez-Gallegos for funding original research on evolutionary dynamics that can be used to transform social systems

- my life partner Karen Mercer for her persistent support, warmth, and generosity, for her help with this manuscript; and for her remarkable ability to catalyze grounded new realizations from my frequent flights of fancy.

It is obvious to me that this book would not have come about without the contributions of every one of these people and from so many more not listed here. This journey has, indeed, been blessed with truly remarkable companions.

Praise for *Reflections on Evolutionary Activism*

I cannot do this inspiring book justice. I see it as a manifesto, a handbook--a gift of love and truth like no other. Tom Atlee, one of a handful of pioneers in the collective intelligence arena, offers all of us a launch point for what he calls evolutionary activism—thought and action that result in conscious evolution of both the individual and society. He stresses that the many tipping point crises that now threaten us (most of our own making) are in fact the perfect environment for calling us out to be creative, innovative, and adaptive. He points to three evolutionary dynamics for guidance: the integration of diversity; a constant alignment with reality; and the harmonization of self-interest with the wellbeing of the whole. A marvelous tour of the emerging evolutionary activist landscape.

ROBERT STEELE,
CEO EARTH INTELLIGENCE NETWORK,
#1 NON-FICTION REVIEWER FOR A MAJOR ONLINE BOOKSELLER
(see his review at EvolutionaryActivism.com)

I always look where Tom Atlee points. His passion for our collective evolution makes him a towering receiver for new possibilities and he serves us all through his brave exploration of powerful ideas and processes.

VICKI ROBIN
CO-AUTHOR OF *YOUR MONEY OR YOUR LIFE*

Once again, Tom Atlee offers a fresh, and penetrating perspective—connecting our understanding of evolution, consciousness, and activism into a new and compelling synthesis for making a difference in today's challenged world. All of us who care about the future of our beloved planet and of our human community need to read this evocative invitation for each of us to become a vehicle for conscious evolution as our unique contribution to the web of life.

JUANITA BROWN AND DAVID ISAACS,
CO-ORIGINATORS, THE WORLD CAFÉ

Having evangelized the marriage of science and religion for years, I am thrilled to see Tom Atlee's offspring of this union: a cosmic Earthactivism grounded in evolutionary science and spirituality. Tom's inspiring poetry and insightful reflections on systemic transformation couldn't be more timely. I urge everyone involved with conscious evolution to give this breakthrough book a serious, joyous read.

MICHAEL DOWD,
AUTHOR OF *THANK GOD FOR EVOLUTION*
endorsed by 6 Nobel laureates and by religious leaders across the spectrum

If a dying Red Giant star could dream what its dust might become, a particularly ambitious star would surely hope to wend its way into the kind of world that Tom Atlee envisions in this book. It is a world safeguarded and guided by inspired and passionate activists who are rooted in reverential awareness of their amazing evolutionary heritage.

CONNIE BARLOW
SCIENCE WRITER AND CREATOR OF
THE ACCLAIMED EPIC OF EVOLUTION EDUCATION WEBSITE
THEGREATSTORY.ORG

Evolutionary activism is an idea whose time has come. In this lucid, engaging book, Tom Atlee, one of today's most compelling and innovative voices for whole-system change, shares from the leading edge of his own learning about how to mobilize our collective wisdom to transform our social systems and give birth to a better world. For anyone interested in the future, this book is a must-read.

CRAIG HAMILTON
FOUNDER, INTEGRALENLIGHTENMENT.COM
AND HOST OF THE GREAT INTEGRAL AWAKENING

Just a moment

what would happen
if all we had
was one universe
one planet
one life
one moment
this?

| ✳ |